PHILADELPHIA GHOST STORIES

by
Charles J. Adams III

Research Team:
David J. Seibold, Lewis B. Gerew II, Sharon M. Gerew
Philadelphia Ghost Hunters Alliance

EXETER HOUSE BOOKS

PHILADELPHIA GHOST STORIES
©Charles J. Adams III

Research Editor: David J. Seibold

For information, write to:
EXETER HOUSE BOOKS
P.O. Box 8134
Reading, Pennsylvania 19603

2005 EDITION

PRINTED IN THE UNITED STATES OF AMERICA

I SBN   1-880683-12-1

TABLE OF CONTENTS

PREFACE

What you are about to read is not a history book.

It is not a book on the occult.

Consider it a travel guide to sites in Philadelphia which lurk "off the beaten track"–*way* off the beaten track.

No matter in what section of the book store you found this volume, I thank you for giving it a look, and hope you will enjoy it.

I've had a wonderful time working on it, and will never forget many of the people and places I was introduced to while working on this, my twentieth book on legends, folklore, and ghost stories.

Put the accent, if you will, on *stories*.

I am not a scholarly folklorist. I am not a historian. I am not a paranormal investigator.

I am but a storyteller.

And as the stories which follow were recorded for retelling, some noteworthy developments–not all unrelated to my chosen genre and the chosen geographical area for this book–unfolded.

It was indeed an interesting year in which to compile a book on the supernatural...in Philadelphia.

An old textile mill in Manayunk and two blocks in Old City Philadelphia were retrofitted to appear as they would have in 1873 for the movie, "Beloved," which was partially filmed in the city.

Based on the 1988 Pulitzer Prize-winning novel by Toni Morrison, the story line of the movie involves a mother who is haunted by the child she murdered to save it from slavery.

Ironically, other scenes for the movie were shot at the (haunted) Landis Valley Museum in Lancaster County.

In the year, the Philadelphia Ghost Hunters Alliance was formed. The Historical Society of Pennsylvania (storehouse of scores of dusty documents related to Philadelphia legends and lore) closed and reopened after extensive renovations.

Independence Hall reopened after a $17 million utilities upgrade.

And, plans were announced that would convert the shuttered (and haunted–see page 111) Philadelphia Navy Yard into a cruise ship terminal and cargo shipbuilding facility.

The General Wayne Inn, said to be the most haunted place in the Philadelphia suburbs, was put on the real estate market. Previous reports claimed as many as 17 spirits, including Edgar Allan Poe's, cavort in the old inn. Its last owner was found dead there in 1996.

England's parliament voted to grant a posthumous pardon to Helen Duncan, who was convicted in 1944 of pretending to raise the spirits of the dead. Duncan, who died in 1956, was jailed for nine months under a 1753 witchcraft law.

And while this book was being written, the Psychic Friends Network filed for bankruptcy. Uh, shouldn't they have foreseen their economic woes?

Perhaps most significantly, there was a changing of the guard at the National Endowment for the Humanities in Washington, D.C.

William R. Ferris Jr. was appointed chairman of the organization. Ferris comes to the N.E.H. as a scholar, but with a specialty in folklore.

The Vicksburg, Mississippi, native holds a master's and PhD in folklore from the University of Pennsylvania.

Finally, it was on the day this page was signed—March 21, 1998, that hundreds of people gathered in a hotel in Gettysburg, Pennsylvania, for the first International Ghost Hunters Society conference ever held in Pennsylvania.

As a symbolic gesture, I concluded this project by driving from Philadelphia to Gettysburg, where I did what I do best....

....told ghost stories.

Charles J. Adams III
Philadelphia and Gettysburg, Pa.
March 21, 1998

Introduction

No city in the United States can claim more historic sites and shrines as can Philadelphia.

When one walks the streets of this magnificent city which is snuggled between the Schuylkill and Delaware rivers, one walks in the steps of Franklin, Jefferson, Washington, and virtually every influential person who ever played a role in the politics, the arts, and the folklore of America.

And, when one walks these streets, one walks among those ghosts of Philadelphia.

I invite you to join me as we venture to places and through neighborhoods of this storied city and introduce you to the spirits that roam in the night and lurk in almost every corner.

We will begin our exploration of the "dark side" of Philadelphia where most visitors begin their visit—in the heart of the historic district and in some of its most famous buildings.

Perhaps the most famous of all is Independence Hall. And, while most people know it only as the birthplace of the United States, some know that it is haunted.

Quite haunted.

Imagine that you are a security guard at Independence Hall. Your job is to help protect an American landmark.

These days, of course, you are aided by electronic

security devices which can detect movement, and the presence of anyone who shouldn't be inside the building when it is closed to the general public.

But...can those electronic gadgets also detect the presence of spirits? Of ghosts?

Imagine again that you are about to close up shop at Independence Hall. The tourists are long gone, the day is done, you're ready to head home, and you make one final sweep of the building before securing it for the night.

You are standing in a corner to the rear of the front door. You know you are alone. Or...are you?

All is very quiet. Quiet, that is, until the sound of footsteps shuffle on the floor of the Long Gallery upstairs. You are certain it is footsteps. Certain, too, that it is the footfall of a stray tourist who somehow was left behind.

You ascend the staircase, cautiously. The footsteps seem to stop at the top of the stairs. You brace yourself for whatever you may encounter.

But nothing can brace you for what you are about to experience.

As you reach the top of the stairs, you sense a chilling feeling. You feel that you are not alone, but you see no one.

Again, and as if directly in front of you, are the footsteps. A musty aroma wafts past you...the air is now icy cold....and not three feet from your face, a cloudy form begins to take shape!

You stand stunned and silent. You have never experienced anything like this in your life, and you have no idea how to handle it.

You are a security guard, but this icy feeling...this musty smell...this emerging form....these are beyond any training and any preparation you have ever had.

Your eyes wide, your feet riveted in place, you watch as the cloudy form seems to take the shape of a human being. A head...shoulders...a torso...as if a massive puff of cigarette smoke was pressed together into a shape, the figure becomes somehow familiar....and then....*and then....*

Poof! It vanishes before your eyes! Gone in an instant!

You breathe for the first time in what seems like hours, and yet it has only been a minute or so. You step back, swallow, wipe your brow. You try to reason with an episode which unfolded from somewhere beyond reason.

You have witnessed...you have come face-to-face...with one of the ghosts of Independence Hall.

I say *ghosts* because over the last century or so, several entities have been reported in the old Pennsylvania State House.

In June, 1994, a tour guide there was in the northwestern corner of Independence Hall, alone (or so he thought), when something caught the corner of his eye.

He said he watched in awe as something—that's the best way he could describe it, *something*—was, again in his words, *working its way through* the main entrance doors.

"It was just filtering through," he said in the 1994 interview. "Then, it took shape. I remember seeing a tri-cornered hat, a long dark-colored coat, white britches or stockings—the expected wardrobe of one of the historical figures who wander around here."

The ranger, who asked that his name not be released, concluded by shrugging his shoulders and saying, "In a flash, it just disappeared....evaporated....vaporized!"

The preceding stories were related by an actual

3

security guard and a park ranger at Independence Hall. To this day, both shudder when they tell their tales.

They don't tell their tales often, or to too many people. You see, the National Park Service tends to shy away from the notion or mention of anything ghostly regarding the properties it maintains.

When research for this book was being compiled, the supervisory park ranger at Independence N.H.S. disavowed any knowledge of, or interest in, any ghosts in the many buildings and many acres of the national treasure.

But, almost any historic site—whether the park service chooses to admit it or not—has its ghost stories.

Another ranger who asked to not be identified said he has often heard stories from historic interpreters who have heard bumps in the night (and in the day) at other park buildings such as Congress Hall and the Bishop White House.

But now, we wander to places beyond the park and meet people who dwell beyond our understanding.

The first of these people we shall encounter is....

Chloris Ingleby

If you're ever down around 260 South 9th Street, you'll come upon a charming rowhome called the Bonaparte House.

Over the years, it's been called the "Meany House," the "Potter House," and the "Price House" as it changed ownership.

It earned its present moniker because Joseph Bonaparte, the older brother of Napoleon, lived there in 1815.

This story would be enhanced much if it could be written that Joseph Bonaparte's ghost dwells within its

4

The ghost of Chloris Ingleby is said to stroll in this alleyway behind the Bonaparte House.

5

stately walls, but that is not true.

There is a ghost in the Bonaparte House...but its name is Chloris. Chloris Ingleby.

A girl of modest means but immodest methods, Chloris Ingleby was supposedly a dancer–and whatever else–in the rowdy taverns along the Delaware River waterfront.

It is said that Chloris lived just down the street from the Bonaparte House, and fell in love with Joseph's steward. That steward, however, was already engaged to a Corsican woman, and fully intended to marry her upon his return to his island homeland.

In her quest to win the heart of the steward, she tried everything, including hiding in the bowels of a ship which was to sail from Philadelphia to Corsica. The steward was to sail on the vessel, and Chloris truly believed she could prove her love on the long voyage and convince the young man to abandon his marriage plans in Corsica.

But, the ship never sailed. And, after several days holed up below decks of the brig on the Philadelphia docks, Chloris was discovered.

Taken into custody as a stowaway, Chloris was imprisoned in a large barn which once stood in the rear of the Bonaparte House.

Somehow, at some time, Chloris seized an opportunity to escape from her confinement. As she fled, she caught the attention of a guard. The guard fired and Chloris fell...dead...in what is now the garden walkway of the Bonaparte House.

And to this day, when the air is still and the moon lights the garden of the old Bonaparte House, the ghost of Chloris Ingleby glides over the ground. More than one resident of the neighborhood has reported seeing the spirit, and some say the moans of her dying moments can still be heard on very quiet nights in that haunted alleyway next to the house.

The Sobbing Spirit of Rittenhouse Square

There is an unfortunate reality in the collection of ghost stories in Philadelphia and, for that matter, anywhere else.

Because those who claim they have seen a ghost are often ridiculed and held in suspicion by less enlightened friends, neighbors, and relatives, they often are unwilling to allow their names used in stories.

And, because their homes, businesses, or properties could be subject to thrill-seeking ghost hunters, they also prefer that specific addresses not be mentioned.

Thus, there is a trade-off when a ghost story researcher seeks eyewitness accounts. While he or she may "get the story," there may have to be an agreement made to not use actual names and locations.

To some readers, that may lessen the credibility of a story. But, it is a necessary evil in the assembling of a ghost story book.

So, although I cannot pinpoint the place or name the name of the owner of the following place, everything you are about to read is true.

The setting is a tree-shaded street, just around the corner from the Curtis Institute, off Rittenhouse Square.

The resident is a professional woman, whose name would be very recognizable to many Philadelphians. It is for that reason that she asked to not be identified.

Her story unfolded in the early 1990s, shortly after she had moved into the large, brick home on the narrow street.

About seven o'clock in the evening, as she sat down at her dining room table to go over some papers and clean up some work leftover from her day in the office, she felt a slight breeze drift over her shoulder and through her long hair.

Distracted, she shook it off and thought little more of it. Then, from a small and empty room just off the dining room, she heard a weak voice say *"Mommy....Mommy...."*

Not yet fully aware of the idiosyncrasies of her new residence, she again tried to brush it off as a sound from somewhere outside. But it was December, and a cold day. The windows were securely shut. The building was ample and solid and little or no sounds could filter through its thick walls.

As she paused, silently, over her papers, she cocked an ear toward that room. There was nothing, not a thing, in the room. She had cleared it an cleaned it in preparation for papering and painting. It was completely empty. It was to become her office after it was renovated.

Again...as if in an echoing whisper...the voice cried out: *"Mommy....Mommy!"*

This time, the voice seemed pained. It seemed, too, as if it was most definitely coming from within that room. And, it seemed that it was coming from a nervous, anguished child.

The woman is tough. Her occupation puts her up against mortals who have been known to cower in her powerful professional presence. Certainly, she must have thought, any disembodied plea from an invisible source could be dealt with.

She gently put down her pen and pushed the chair back from the table. It was time to investigate the source of the sound.

8

Maybe, she thought, it was not "Mommy" at all, and not at all a child's voice. Maybe, she hoped, it was a natural or mechanical sound she only interpreted as a word, and a voice.

As she made her way slowly to the little room, again she heard...."*Mommy!*"

This time, the voice and the word were all too clear. This time, it was very evident that the voice was coming from one particular corner of the empty room.

Determined more than ever to get to the bottom of the mystery, the woman stopped and directed all her nervous attention to the room.

She remembers that the silence was almost eerie as she awaited another utterance. Surely, it would come. Surely, there would be a logical explanation for it all.

And surely, the phantom voice reappeared. But this time, it seemed to be crying and stammering.

"*M-M-Mommy*" is all it said. And, all it would ever say, any time again.

The woman waited five, ten, fifteen more minutes, frozen in place near the doorway to the little room.

Nothing. Not a sound. No voice.

She was shaken by the encounter, but at the same time was spurred on to find out what might have generated the ghostly word.

Never a true believer in the spirit world, the woman was nonetheless open-minded enough to accept the possibility that she shared her new home with a ghost.

But this ghost, if indeed there was one, seemed so young, so innocent, so alone.

It was by a quirk of fate that the mystery may have been solved.

9

Less than a week after the presence made itself known in that little room, the woman happened to meet a neighbor—a gent who had lived on the block for the better part of 50 years.

In a casual discussion, unprompted by the woman, the neighborhood elder began to spin yarns about the block and those who have come and gone over the years.

The woman was amused by most of his ramblings, but her attitude changed quickly when the talk turned to her house, and to one particular room, and to one particular former resident thereof.

It seemed that in the early 1950s, there lived in that house a mother, a father, and a little boy.

That little boy led a short and sorrowful life. Deformed and stricken with a severe illness, he spent all of his three short years on earth in that small room, just off the dining room.

And it was in that little room, the old man said, that the little boy died....in the arms....of his *mommy*.

The woman who had purchased that house, and had heard the plaintive call from that room nodded and winced when the man mentioned one more anecdote about that unfortunate little boy.

The old gentlemen chuckled and dismissed what he was about to tell her, but the woman listened intently.

Some folks who lived in that house after the little boy died there, the man said, claimed that his ghost was still inside. With a wave of his hand and a quick change to another subject, the old man brushed aside that claim.

But, the woman could only offer a weak smile and a false nod of agreement.

She knew better!

A city as old and as important as Philadelphia is bound to have its share of enduring—and sometimes endearing—legends. The following is one of the more fascinating.

The Walking Statue of Pennsylvania Hospital

The classic architecture and lovely grounds of the Pennsylvania Hospital abound with historical lore, and there's even a legend or two down at the oldest hospital in the United States.

You name the prominent Philadelphian in the earliest years of the city, and they have passed through (and sometimes *passed away* in) Pennsylvania Hospital.

In its main building are many priceless works of art, the first operating room in the country, and a chair once owned by William Penn.

But it is a *statue* of William Penn in the hospital's lovely gardens along Pine Street which has spawned a very strange piece of Philadelphia folklore.

Nobody's really sure how old the statue might be. An article in the Philadelphia *Bulletin* in 1905 told of repairs to be done to the statue, and noted that it was, at that time, at least 130 years old.

The article claimed the statue was first mentioned in a letter from Benjamin Franklin to a friend.

The statue of Penn somehow found its way into a London salvage warehouse where it was noticed and retrieved by Penn's son, John. He donated the statue to the hospital in 1804.

Since the early 19th century, a story has circulated that on certain nights, a ghostly figure steps down from the

The Walking Statue of William Penn at the Pennsylvania Hospital.

pedestal of the statue and strolls through the grounds of the hospital.

There are several versions of the tale. One times the statue's stroll to the night of a full moon. Another claims it walks on the stroke of midnight on New Year's Eve.

The Philadelphia *Press* noted in a story in 1884 a legend that the statue spirit made its journey whenever the State House (Independence Hall) clock struck six in the evening.

"Nurses brought children from afar to watch it," the *Press* reported. "On summer evenings expectant little faces peered through the railing of the fence on Pine Street.

"Little hearts beat fast at the first stroke of six. Five...ten...twenty minutes...even a half hour, the watchers would wait. Though obliged to turn away disappointed, their faith still remained."

One morning, the article continued, the statue was found face down, in the walkway in front of the hospital door.

"Older members of the community said that the storm which had raged high during the night, had caused the accident," the reported wrote.

"But the children knew better...storm indeed!"

In an extension of the "walking statue" legend at Pennsylvania Hospital, some even say it is the ghost of William Penn himself—his energy eternally attached to his effigy—which detaches from the statue and performs the occasional nocturnal perambulation down along Pine Street.

Penn's statue is not the only restless monument in the city.

A late 19th century legend had it that every Easter morning, the bronze likeness of Ben Franklin detached itself from its nook above the door of the old Philadelphia Library and danced down the sidewalks of town!

Exactly which statue might strut its stuff remains a matter of speculation. There is a statue of Franklin above Library Hall on South 5th Street, but it is a replacement, added when the library was reconstructed in the 1950s.

The weatherbeaten original, and presumably the "dancing" statue, was removed to the Library Company building at 1314 Locust Street.

If Dr. Franklin's effigy no longer prances along the pavements, perhaps his very ghost does remain in the city in which he died and is buried.

The Ghostly Mr. Franklin

No book about Philadelphia ghosts would be complete without a story about the rumored wraith of one of the city's true legends.

Indeed, the very house in which Franklin spent his last years remains only in ghostly form.

Demolished in 1812, the home and print shop designed and built by Franklin once stood behind a row of tenants' houses in the 300 block of Market Street.

Visitors may peek through glass into the privy, onto scant foundations and walls, and other features still visible below the modern paved plaza known as Franklin Court.

Although the exact dimensions of the building are not known, the National Park Service in 1973 commissioned architects to construct a "ghost" of steel beams which rise to form an approximation of the shape and dimensions of the original structure.

Does Ben Franklin's spirit stroll Franklin Court? Folks in the museum under the plaza won't say. But legend has it

14

that his restless soul has been heard from in several other parts of the city.

It was Franklin himself who proposed the first formal subscription library in Philadelphia (and the country). The site of its first building is now Library Hall (the library of the American Philosophical Society), and it was there that at least one employee reported a close encounter with old Ben himself.

Franklin had been in his grave several years when a cleaning lady described in one 19th century account as "a colored woman of unquestioned respectability" claimed to have bumped into his ghost while she and her daughter were tidying things up in the early morning hours.

A feature in the Philadelphia *Press* newspaper in 1884 reported the episode:

"As he took no notice of the two women and never interfered with them, they grew used to seeing him. He went his way and they theirs.

"One morning, when mother and daughter were hard at work, as luck would have it, Franklin, his arms full of books, came to the case, in front of when the latter was scrubbing away.

"She moved to make room for him, but encumbered as she was, with pails and brushes, she was not quick enough and he, in his ghostly nearsightedness or impatience, pushed against her with unghostlike violence and nearly tumbled her over, so she said."

But now, let us search the streets of Philadelphia for one particular shadowy form which could well materialize out along the Wissahickon, down along the Schuylkill, right around the corner, or.....*just over your shoulder.*

Here He Pondered, Weak and Weary...

Philadelphia has spawned many fine writers who have delved into the genres of the supernatural and horror.

Charles Brockden Brown (1771-1810) has been recognized by some as the first full-time American author. And, his novel, *Wieland*, is likewise considered to be the first true American novel.

Wieland is set in a mansion along the Schuylkill River, and Brown populated the eerie place with a young man who is driven by "voices" to slay his family, a psychic older man, and any number of other strange characters.

George Lippard (1822-1854) and Robert Montgomery Bird (1806-1854) also touched on the bizarre.

And, while he had no real connections to the city, a certain Scottish writer spent time in Philadelphia and did major work on his novel while he stayed in the Bellevue Stratford Hotel.

That writer: Bram Stoker. That novel: *Dracula*.

Perhaps the homegrown spirits of Lippard, Brown, and Bird remain somewhere on the streets of Philadelphia. And a bit of Stoker's energies really do remain here—albeit not in spirit form. The Rosenbach Museum & Library on Delancey Place has in its collection nearly 100 pages of notes on vampirism and werewolves, penned in the writer's hand on Bellevue Stratford stationery.

But another legendary writer may have left a psychic imprint on Philadelphia, and what an imprint it could be.

Beware, ladies and gentlemen, of the ghost of....*Edgar Allan Poe.*

It would not be an overstatement to say that this city was the setting for some of Poe's most delightful, and most

Edgar Allan Poe lived in this home near 7th and Spring Garden Sts.

desperate days.

It was here where he drew inspiration for such classics as "The Tell-Tale Heart" and "Murders of the Rue Morgue."

It was here that he threatened suicide...was detained in jail....and began a steady and swift decline into depression and delusion.

And, it is in here where, some believe, his ghost remains.

Poe's footfalls may remain in any of several places known to have been the haunts, so to speak, of the legendary author.

His first visit to Philadelphia was as a 20-year old aspiring writer when, in 1829, he stayed over at the Indian Queen Hotel, 15 S. 4th Street.

Nine years later, an impoverished Poe and his beloved cousin/wife Virginia, moved to the city and took up residence at 202 Arch Street.

It was said that they would survive for long stretches on little more that "bread and molasses."

Frustrated with his foundering literary career and forced to literally beg and borrow enough money to pay the meager rent, Poe eventually solicited officials for a federal job in Philadelphia, but failed in that effort.

How, we can only imagine, would American literature have been changed had Poe become a Federal bureaucrat?

Later in 1838, Poe moved to another tiny house on 16th Street near Locust. His writings began to attract some attention.

Unfortunately, Poe's erratic behavior and presumed drinking problems also attracted the ire of those who would be his benefactors.

Still, his output of work in Philadelphia continued, and he circulated among the city's leading writers and artists.

As Poe prowled the streets of this publishing mecca, he managed to sell stories to magazines and newspapers, review plays and books, and meet influential contemporaries. Poe was known to gather with other writers at the old Falstaff Hotel on 6th Street above Chestnut.

In 1840, Poe is known to have traveled to Andalusia, the estate of Nicholas Biddle, where the writer asked the banker for assistance.

If any energy from that era remains, it may be very strong down on Chestnut Street above 4th, where two legends crossed paths in 1842.

Just after his return from a visit to Eastern State Penitentiary, Charles Dickens met with Edgar Allan Poe in the United States Hotel.

Oh, to have been in that room on that occasion!

Later in 1842, Poe moved again, into what was described as a small but comfortable home in the rural outskirts-of the city—to Fairmount. His residence was where 2502 Fairmount Street stands today.

From there, Poe often strolled in, and wrote about, the stunningly beautiful Wissahickon Creek valley.

Life was getting a bit easier for Poe by that time. In 1843 he, his wife/cousin, his mother-in-law/aunt, and their cat, Catterina, moved into a sturdy "lean-to" on the west side of 234 N. 7th St. in the suburb of Spring Garden.

Now in the middle of the city, that property is the Edgar Allan Poe National Historic Site.

The odd family there drew the attention of neighbors, such as this from the recollections of a local school girl:

"In the mornings the two women would be generally watering the flowers.

"They seemed always cheerful and happy, and I could hear Mrs. Poe's laugh before I turned the corner.

"You would notice how clean and orderly everything looked."

Another neighbor noted that while the three lived in poverty, they were proud and kept their property quite clean. And, "Eddy," as he was called, cut a memorable figure.

"Dozens of times have I seen him pass my father's windows going down Seventh Street into the city," the neighbor wrote.

"He wore a Spanish cloak; they, at that time, were much used instead of overcoats. I was always impressed with the grave and thoughtful aspect of his face. He looked to be much older than I now know him to have been.

"Though little over thirty, he had the appearance of middle age. To his neighbors, his name meant very little. It was not after 'The Raven' was published that we knew him as a literary figure.

"Then, we felt sorry we had not taken more notice of him."

Poe continued to write, embarked on a lecture tour, and gained some of the respect he sought. Still, he fought insecurity, poverty, and emotional distress.

In 1843, a writer described Poe as "A pale, gentlemanly looking personage with a quick, piercing, restless eye, and a very broad and peculiarly shaped forehead.

"He would occasionally utter some brilliant jests. His fine analytical powers, together with his bitter and apparently candid style, made him the terror of dunces and the evil spirit of wealthy blockheads, who create books without possessing brains."

His career on an upswing, Poe left Philadelphia in 1844 for new opportunities in New York City.

But, he would pass through this city again, staying over at Arbuckle's Western Hotel, 288 Market St., in 1847, and for the last time in July, 1849.

That visit proved to provide the most startling tales of Poe's personal life, and reveal the demons which bedeviled him until his final moments alive.

The first demon struck at the rail depot when he arrived in Philadelphia just three months before his death. He claimed that a valise which contained the texts of his two lectures was either misplaced or stolen at the train station.

And not long after stepping off the train, Poe was arrested and detained for a few hours at the county prison, Moyamensing, at 10th and Reed Sts. The charge: drunkenness.

The last chapter in Poe's association with Philadelphia opened on July 3, 1849, when Poe was given refuge by friend John Sartain in his engraving studio at 728 Sansom Street.

Poe and Sartain became acquainted when Poe was editor of *Graham's* magazine in 1843 (for the salary of $800 a year)

In later writings which seem to be at odds with other research, Sartain described his guest as "pale and haggard, with a wild and frightened expression in his eyes." He said Poe had told him he felt someone was trying to kill him.

Poe asked Sartain for a razor to shave his mustache—figuring that his assassins, real or imagined, would not recognize him.

Sartain tried to oblige the obviously deranged Poe, but having no razor, he satisfied Poe's request by clipping his mustache with scissors.

And then, it was off to the Fairmount Waterworks and Reservoir for a therapeutic stroll along the Schuylkill. But before they departed, Sartain loaned Poe a pair of slippers. Poe's own shoes were worn through the soles.

And while he feared for Poe's sanity, Sartain would

John Sartain

provide him with what he hoped would be a pleasant stay. But the highest, most horrid drama in Poe's last days in the city was yet to unfold.

"After tea, it now being dark," Sartain wrote in his book, *Reminiscences of a Very Old Man*, I saw [Poe] preparing to go out; and on my asking him where he was going, he said, 'To the Schuylkill.' I told him I would go, too—it would be pleasant in the moonlight later—and he

The Fairmount Water Works at around the turn of the century—note the reservoir on the hill where the Museum of Art now stands.

offered no objection."

John Sartain truly feared for Poe's life. When they walked along the river, and on the Waterworks ledges, he kept between Poe and the river.

As the two climbed to the rim of the reservoir which was located where the art museum is today, Sartain positioned himself between Poe and the edge.

"I kept on his left side," Sartain wrote, "and on approaching the foot of the bridge guided him off to the right by a gentle pressure until we reached the lofty flight of steep wooden steps which ascended almost to the top of the reservoir."

"It came into my mind that Poe might possibly, in a sudden fit of frenzy, leap freely forth with me in his arms into the black depth below, so I was watchful and kept on my guard," Sartain later wrote.

Poe babbled incessantly. He told Sartain that while in a detainment cell at Moyamensing he had a hallucination in which his mother-in-law was being dismembered. He spoke of "weird and fantastic" visions.

A few days later, Poe wrote a rambling, frightening letter to his mother-in-law back in New York: "I have been so ill. I have had the cholera or spasms quite as bad, and can now hardly hold the pen. But I must die. I have no desire to live since I have done 'Eureka.' I have been taken to prison once since I came here for getting drunk; but *then*, I was not!"

Poe left Philadelphia later in July, visited Richmond, and was passing through Baltimore on the way back through Philadelphia and then home to New York when, on October 7, 1849, in a hospital room in Baltimore, Edgar Allan Poe fought his last demons.

After telling nurses the best thing anyone could do was to blow his brains out with a pistol...after saying he was ready to "sink into the earth"....after casting his eyes toward the ceiling of the room and quietly uttering, "Lord help my poor soul," Edgar Allan Poe died.

Does the ghost of Edgar Allan Poe haunt Philadelphia to this day? Some say it does. A well-respected trance-medium has long believed that Poe's energy remains, trapped in a spiral of psychic energy, within the confines of the old Fairmount Water Works along the Schuylkill.

The researcher speaks of a troubled, confused spirit which has emerged to unsuspecting visitors as a fleeting figure along the walkway between the art museum and the Water Works.

Eastern Penitentiary, Philadelphia, Pa.

An early 20th century view of Eastern State Penitentiary.

The Ghosts of Eastern State Penitentiary

In the Fairmount section of Philadelphia, is what could be considered the "Alcatraz of the East," the magnificent, stabilized ruin of Eastern State Penitentiary.

Eerie, foreboding, definitely not for the claustrophobic, Eastern State is at once decaying, dying, and a reprehensible representative of death and depravation.

It also, in the late 1990s, became one of the most sought-out tourist attractions in Philadelphia.

In 1829, when the massive Gothic monstrosity of a building opened, it had plenty of running water when the rest of the city did not. It had a flush toilet in every cell when the president of the nation used an outhouse. It had a form deemed so efficient that some 300 prisons around the world were built on plans based on architect John Haviland's design.

The hub-and-spoke configuration allowed guards in a central rotunda to look over all activities in all cellblocks, which fanned out from the middle.

Some background on what went on inside its 30-foot high, 12-foot thick walls will amplify the almost audible screams of agony and anguish that seem to reverberate eternally throughout the dusty, crusty cellblocks.

The corrective system used at E.S.P. from 1829 to 1913 came to be called The Pennsylvania System.

Actually, it was a *Quaker* system of simple, strict, solitary confinement. Drawn up in 1787 by a committee which met in Ben Franklin's home, the concept of isolation for punishment also put the word *penitence* in penitentiary.

Prisoners' cells were equipped with a toilet, table, bunk, and Bible. Inmates were locked in all but 30 minutes in the morning and 30 minutes in the evening. Even those half-hour releases were spent in isolated exercise plots outside the cells. There were no visits, no interaction with other inmates.

Only one beam of daylight (from what was called "The Eye of God") slithered through a slot in the ceiling.

The system was so well known worldwide that when Dickens made his visit to America, he said he wanted to see only two sights—Niagara Falls and Eastern State.

The writer was quick to criticize the harsh conditions at the prison, and prison officials were quick to retort, saying Dickens had been conned by the cons.

The most expensive building in the United States when it was built, Eastern (also known locally as the "Cherry Hill" Penitentiary) underwent sweeping reform in 1913, as the structure designed to house 250 inmates was swelling to an

A grim view of a cellblock at Eastern State Penitentiary, 1998.

eventual population of 1,700. The system was termed inhumane and the prison was refurbished.

Al Capone spent a year (1929) at the prison. Willie Sutton escaped (1945) from it. The prison finally closed in 1971.

The legends and lore of the old penitentiary are legion.

So, too, are its ghosts.

In Cellblock 12, several visitors have reported the hollow, distant sound of evil, cackling women echoing in certain cells.

In the "six block," volunteers have seen shadowy forms gliding along walls.

But of the many graphic reports of ghostly activity at E.S.P., the story of a middle-age locksmith is perhaps the most powerful and most frightening.

Not long ago, the man was alone there, at dusk, in "four block" (Cell block #4), performing routine restoration work.

At one particular moment, he was removing a 140-year old lock from the door of an abandoned cell when he encountered an energy so incredible and so powerful that to this day, he shudders when he recalls his introduction to the ghosts of Eastern State Penitentiary.

It was as if that locksmith somehow possessed the key which opened the portal to Eastern State's tortured past—and was ushered through that ghastly getaway by the phantoms who dwell in those cells.

Faces in the walls....a glowing, floating rock...a foggy, steamy, form which seemed to beckon....

These images were only *part* of the man's encounter with the unknown in Cell block 4 that night.

He was physically transported into a nether world by a

Time has taken its toll on the cells at Eastern State Penitentiary.

tidal wave of energy upon which as many as 100 ghosts spiraled.

In what might be described as an "out of body" experience, the locksmith felt drawn not only *to*, but *into*, the horrible supernatural stew.

One spirit seemed to dominate and rise above all others. It rose as the form of a man, with three rings of steam, or mist swirling around it. But within a short time, others...hundreds...of bizarre forms materialized.

He describes his emotions at the time in weird and confounding terms—"It was as if I was inside a microwave oven," he says. But then, there were moments when, he recalls, it was as if he was "standing buck naked in a sandstorm at the North Pole!"

So confounding and confusing was the episode that the locksmith was riveted in place, unable to move, as spirits cried from every chamber and wall of "four block."

He could do nothing but stand petrified amid the ghosts—or at least *some* of the ghosts—which haunt that very special....and very *haunted* place.

Philadelphia's First Ghost Hunter

The book you are about to read is the first published collection of true ghost stories and legends of the city of Philadelphia.

This is not to say, however, that others have not compiled and shared some of these stories, and many other ghostly tales of the City of Brotherly Love.

Probably the earliest "ghost hunter" in Philadelphia was Elizabeth Robins, a writer for the Philadelphia *Press* newspaper in the late 19th century.

In January 1884, Robins wrote a story, "Our Own

Ghosts," in which she related details of several haunted places in the city and solicited more stories.

The result was a followup story under the same heading as the first, and a fascinating early tour through haunted Philadelphia.

Ms. Robins' introduction was a precursor of any words we could offer:

"That Philadelphia is a city so noted for its aristocracy and its old houses, should have ghost stories, is a matter of course."

In her assessment of Philadelphia folklore and its peoples' propensity for the supernatural, Robins cited the group most often associated with the founding of what has been called the "Quaker City."

"The Quakers," she wrote, "who, by making religion a mystery, promoted faith in shadows. Whatever Quakerism may be now, it was, in its early days, mysticism of the first order. Its very basis is belief in the activity made manifest of spiritual agents."

A short review of Ms. Robins' stories will serve to whet the appetites of readers of this volume, and send would-be ghost hunters out to track down any ambient energies which may remain at the sites.

Then, as now, chroniclers of haunted places were obliged to trade anonymity for a good ghost story.

While the credibility of a particular story may seem to suffer when the exact address and correct name of the place and persons affected by the ghostly goings-on are changed, it is sometimes the price need to be paid just to secure the story.

In this book, several names and locations have been

changed, so as to protect the property and the integrity of the contributor.

Rest assured, however, that no story in this volume has been fabricated.

Elizabeth Robins apparently faced the same trade-off as she gathered her stories.

She wrote, for example about a haunting which was, in her words, "so modern in date were in truth wiser not to identify it."

Robins said only that it was on "one of the thoroughfares which has a place in the old rhyming list of Philadelphia streets, nearer the Schuylkill than the Delaware."

Servants were bedeviled by horrible sounds which came from the coal bin and furnace, and by a mysterious wraith who eventually sent them fleeing the house in utter fear.

One passage in Ms. Robins' account provides details of a chilling encounter, as well as a glimpse into her writing style.

"At the witching hour of night, the four walls of the servants' sleeping-room would seem to draw closer and closer together, until the terrified women lay quaking in their beds, expecting every minute to be their last.

"Verily, their tormenters savored of the inquisition. Once in a long, long while the ruling spirit—a tall figure, enveloped in white drapery, coming out of nowhere and vanishing as quickly into no—whither—appeared in the midst of the unnerved domestics, who, unable to bear this last horror, shook the dust of the house off their feet and departed from it forever."

And now, returning like literary ghosts themselves, some summaries from the 1884 writings of Philadelphia's first ghost hunter, Elizabeth Robins.

The Garden Ghost of Fourth and Race

The northwest corner of Fourth and Race Streets is now a portion of the Franklin Square park at the Pennsylvania end of the Ben Franklin Bridge, catty-corner from the U.S. Mint.

It was once the site of the Penington Mansion—a handsome home festooned with pleasant gardens.

For many years, neighbors reported seeing the ghostly image of a young woman—presumed to have been the deceased daughter of Mr. and Mrs. Penington—strolling at midnight through the gardens, tending its beauteous bounty with a watering pot.

Not far away, along Arch Street near Second, another spirit made its presence known with eerie sounds and a tendency to shatter any glassware which came its way.

The "Hag of Pine Street"

On the south side of Pine Street, between Sixth and Seventh, one particular home was the scene of frightening episodes related to the ghost of an old woman who had died inside and whose spirit had refused to leave.

Muffled moans and stifled shrieks could be heard inside the building, and many passers-by swore they saw the pale, wrinkled face of the woman in a window.

There was also a report of what became known as the "Hag of Pine Street" walking in ghostly shadows on that block.

The house became so feared that no one would purchase it after the old woman died.

Eventually, a black woman named Betsy Bassett dared to move in.

But Betsy had a plan, as Ms. Robins reported:

"At first she was a little worried by her fellow boarder, but not for a moment daunted. She did not take flight—not she!

"She did something wiser. She sent for the conjuring man, a famous voodoo of those days.

'And he, by ways that were dark and arts that were vile, disposed of that ghost forever.

"The unhappy spirit no longer walks in the old homestead."

Or does it? Some say the "Hag of Pine Street" can still be seen, and her cackling heard, on certain nights.

The Unknown Ghost of St. Peter's

A couple blocks east is the beautiful St. Peter's Church and its classic burial ground.

In that graveyard are the remains of the known—Stephen Decatur, Benjamin Chew, Charles Willson Peale; and the unknown—several Indian chiefs who died in the 1793 smallpox epidemic.

And in that shadowy, atmospheric graveyard is a ghost or two.

It could indeed be called the "Unknown Ghost," as its identity has never been established.

What has been established is that the spirit is usually seen just before dawn, walking very stiffly and quietly between rows of weathered tombstones, never turning its head, and never wavering from its arrow-straight course until it vanishes near a church yard wall.

That ghost was first mentioned in writings as early as 1834, but the story's, and the ghost's whereabouts ever since are, well, unknown!

34

• PHILADELPHIA GHOST STORIES •

Hysterics and a Haunting on Eleventh Street

One of the most disastrous events in the history of Philadelphia was the yellow fever epidemic of 1793.

It was not only a threat to the people of Philadelphia, but imperiled the young nation itself. As the Grim Reaper of death trod the streets dealing its evil fever, it took with it hundreds of souls. Federal officials feared that the infrastructure of the United States bureaucracy may be claimed by the fever, and hastily moved the seat of government to the the country suburb of Germantown.

When the plague spread to that settlement, the capital functions were moved even farther into the Pennsylvania frontier, to York.

Several ghost stories are rooted in the great epidemic of 1793, but none as sad as one which can be traced to a long-since forgotten house on the east side of 11th Street, between Walnut and Spruce.

It is said that a man who lived in that block had contracted the dreaded disease. His neighbors, believing he had died from it, boarded up his doors and windows with his body inside. They felt by doing that, the fever would be contained inside.

In reality, the man did not die. He regained his health and quickly realized that he had been imprisoned within his own home by the hysterical neighbors.

Weak but aware, the man struggled to push out a wooden board which had been nailed to a second floor window. But as he pushed the board away, he fell through the window to the sidewalk, and died of a broken back.

After the yellow fever had run its course and Philadelphia was once again livable, people passing by that vacant house on 11th Street could hear painful moans and muffled screams.

Several reported seeing the agonized face of a man peering from the same second story window from which the ill-fated yellow fever "victim" had plunged.

The Robins Legacy

Elizabeth Robins likely had no idea that her writings would be remembered more than a century after they were printed in a Philadelphia newspaper.

But anyone who today traipses the streets of this noble city in search of the supernatural owes a debt of gratitude to the writer who captured, in 1884, literary snapshots of the very earliest Philadelphia Ghost Stories.

Leah, the Quaker Ghost
of Washington Square

William Penn incorporated five public squares into his plan for Philadelphia. As Quakers frowned on naming things after people, the squares were simply named for their geographic positions in Penn's rigid grid: Centre, Southwest, Southeast, Northeast, and Northwest.

Upon Centre Square now rises City Hall. Upon Northeast Square rises the ramps of the Ben Franklin Bridge.

Southwest is now Rittenhouse Square, and Southeast is Washington Square.

Owing to the slash of the Benjamin Franklin Parkway and the flow of traffic into and out of it, what was Northwest Square is now more commonly called "Logan Circle."

Long before these plots of green became firmly established as parks, they served many functions.

And even today, every one of them serves as a setting for ghost stories.

Another writer who recorded some of the early ghost stories in Philadelphia was John F. Watson. In volume one of his 1887 "Annals of Philadelphia," Watson ever so briefly tantalized the reader with a paragraph of paranormal sites which dated back as far as the Revolutionary War.

Watson recounted well-known haunted houses with a tantalizing alacrity: "...on the northeast corner of Walnut and Fifth Streets....Emlen's House, at the southwest corner of Noble and Second Streets...Naglee's House, far out Second

Street, near the ropewalk, where a man was to be seen hanging without a head...the Masters' place, out North Fourth Street...".

Watson also recalled a pre-Revolution story about a black carriage which could be seen and heard on the streets of town at midnight, driven by a faceless spirit.

And, he mentioned, if ever so briefly, a ghost which walks the perimeter of Centre Square.

That ghost, Watson said, was the victim of murder by what Watson called "the five wheelbarrow men."

It seems that "wheelbarrow men" were convicts who were sent out from prison to toil on public works as a "Chain Gang."

On one occasion, a gang of five chained prisoners attacked and killed an innocent homeowner in the yard of a house just off Centre Square.

The murderers later met their deaths at the end of ropes on a common gallows on that square, where City Hall now stands.

Later, what is now Logan Circle was a public hanging ground.

As late as February 7, 1823, the public execution of convicted killer William Gross was carried out there.

Both Logan Circle and Washington Square also hold within their soil the bones of thousands of bodies, ranging from both British and American Revolutionary War soldiers to Indians to paupers, vagrants, thieves, and yellow fever victims.

Logan Circle was chiefly a Potter's Field, where unidentified or unclaimed corpses were unceremoniously interred.

Does "Leah" prowl this corner of Washington Square?

Washington Square also served as a burying ground for the indigent, but it has a more honorable role as the final resting place for an estimated 2,000 soldiers from both armies of the Revolution. A memorial to the Unknown Soldier of the Revolutionary War is situated on the western end of the square.

And, Washington Square has a ghost.

She is Leah, and her story is rooted in a legend which has survived more than two centuries.

There was a time when grave diggers and even superintendents of these "Potter's Fields" were known to supplement their income by turning over bodies to medical students and physicians for research.

Late in the 19th century, a strange woman known only as "Leah" could be spotted, in the dead of night, prowling Washington Square as a self-appointed protector of the dead and keeper of the graves there.

Described in one account as a "weird and spectral Quakeress," Leah would be seen cloaked in a dark blanket, bent over by age and making eye contact with no one.

It was her presence that kept many a prospective grave-robber from the square, according to the story handed down over the generations.

There came a time when Leah's mortal figure no longer came to call on Washington Square. As mysteriously as she lived, she died. Her true identity, and indeed any substantive details of her life passed with little notice but to those who had witnessed her graveyard strolls.

Something very odd happened after death halted Leah's eerie assignment on Washington Square. It seems that her death had really only *interrupted* her walks between the

40

graves.

For many years, folks passing through Washington Square have reported seeing the hunched, cloaked figure of a woman gliding ghostly through the park.

The most recent sighting of what could well be the ghost of Leah was by none other than a Philadelphia police detective who, for what should be obvious reasons, asked that his name not be used.

"I was walking through Washington Square on a rather cold November morning, as I did quite often from my house on South 6th to the Round House.

"I stopped for a few minutes to pour some coffee from a plastic cup into my insulated jug, and out over toward Walnut Street I saw an old woman rustling through the leaves.

"It really wasn't anything unusual, I figured it was just some bag lady wandering through the park.

"But something looked odd about this particular bag lady. She seemed somehow out of place. I mean, there was something about her that didn't look right. Maybe it was the cop in me, but I walked closer.

"Here's where it gets weird. I looked closely at her and the more I tried to get a make on her face, the more trouble I had *seeing* any face. Honest-to-God, it was as if there was no face, no head, under the blanket that was wrapped over her shoulders!

"I tried not to be noticeable to her. I kept my distance and kind of staked her out. But the strangest thing was yet to come."

The detective paused, shook his head, and took a deep breath as he told his story at a table in a center city restaurant. Having composed himself, he continued.

"You're going think I'm some sort of whacko when I tell you what happened next, and you'll also know why I don't want any of my friends or any bigwigs on the force to know who's talking here...

"But I'll swear on a stack of bibles that as I watched that old lady, she just up and disappeared. Poof! Vanished–right before my eyes.

"Now, I've seen a lot of strange things in my days, but this was the strangest. I stood there like I had been punched in the face. That woman, or whatever, just flat out disappeared!"

The police detective had given his story with no knowledge of the legend of Leah. He had been referred to the author of this book by a resident of an apartment building on the south side of Washington Square, and neither that individual nor the detective knew of the "weird, spectral Quakeress."

After the detective told his story, we informed him of Leah.

He was stunned. "Well, I'll tell you," he said, "I never believed in ghosts before, but with what I saw and what you just told me, maybe there's something to it.

"All I know is that whenever I walk through the square–and I do quite often–I keep looking for that same woman, or whatever. I never saw her after that one time...and maybe I don't really want to!"

The Jilted Spirit

The graffiti-gorged and trash-strewn wasteland around Germantown Avenue and Cecil B. Moore Avenue (nee Columbia Avenue) appears to harbor only the ghosts of North Philadelphia East's once thriving manufacturing enterprises.

But could it be that a spirit from the past still inhabits that hardscrabble corner?

The baseline for this story is in about 1870, and in what was a Methodist Church.

The ghost is Clara, and the tale is sad.

Clara Russell and James Leslie were both teachers, and in the course of their workdays at school, their professional admiration for one another melted into a personal relationship which led to James asking for Clara's hand in marriage.

The effervescent Clara accepted readily. The date was set, and the marriage was to take place at the home of the bride not far from the church.

The wonderful day arrived and Clara's family was eager for the ceremony. Clara was bedecked in her bridal finery, her attendants were at hand, but when the appointed time for the exchange of vows came, a very vital ingredient was missing.

James Leslie.

As time passed, the young woman's joy was sapped by

the disappearance of her beloved James.

Friends and relatives tried to comfort the would-be bride, but as darkness fell and all realized that the marriage would not take place, Clara erupted in fits of despair.

Nothing could be done to console her, and Clara's health deteriorated as quickly as her mental state.

Within a few weeks, she learned that James not only had rejected her at the altar, he had also found another woman and had eloped to a distant state.

Now totally consumed in grief, Clara withered away and died on a summer's day.

She was put to rest in a vault under the floor of the old Methodist Church.

Not soon after Clara's burial, as the church sexton went about his business on a particularly long work day, the astonished and petrified man was distracted by a shadowy form which crossed in front of him just as the clock struck midnight.

It was the form of a woman, dressed in a wrinkled wedding gown. Her face was pale, her hair in a wild mess.

The sexton stood riveted in place as the ghost seemed to clap its hands and cry, "James, oh James, come back!"

Soon, word spread around the neighborhood of Clara's disconsolate spirit. Other eyewitnesses confirmed that they, too, had seen it on its midnight quest for redemption.

Even after the church had been turned into a social hall in the late 19th century, attendees at various functions—some totally unaware of Clara's story—said they saw that same sad figure and heard it cry out for its cruel lover.

The Cryptic Card

Exactly what happened and what its meaning may be remains a mystery to a South Philadelphia man who experienced some rather disturbing events in a charming row house in Fairmount, not far from the Philadelphia Museum of Art.

It was 1993 when Ross (he asked we not use his last name) and a friend found the place and found it was just what they were looking for. The rent was reasonable, the landlord was friendly and had recently restored the place, and the location was perfect.

"It seemed like such a good deal," Ross said, "that we later ended up joking that the house must be haunted!"

Oops!

"We were approved by the landlord," Ross continued, "and in a few weeks, moved in.

"Then, the oddness began.

"Much of it was trivial—a close friend stopping by and asking an unsolicited question about the house being haunted, a radical change in the behavior of our cat, who began doing somersaults; and a creeping, tired feeling I'd sometimes feel upon passing through the dining room.

"Some of it, though, was less trivial. My roommate and I each saw a quick glimpse of people in our rooms on our first morning in the house. Both of us, out of the corner of our eyes, saw them. In her room was a woman in a red dress. In my room was a man in an old-fashioned sailor suit."

Ross added that he and his roommate were at once "thrilled and terrified" that they may have shared their new residence with ghosts. "So," he said, "very soon every creaking door or dripping faucet became the work of 'the ghost."

The disturbances calmed down over the ensuing weeks, but on an afternoon in August, Ross discovered something that continues to baffle him to this day.

"I was digging behind the living room mantel with a coat hanger in an attempt to recover a $20 bill which had slipped down behind it.

"I began to pull up weird things. One was a ragged piece of paper with a one-cent stamp attached. I began to pull out more and more bits of what appeared to have been a post card, and when I pieced them together, I found it was dated August 9, 1909.

"The card had a picture of a local observatory on one side, and a short, cryptic message on the other. The name was Charles Strohm—and according to research I did later, there was indeed a family named Strohm living at the address in 1909—and the message read, 'How about last Saturday'.

"The piece of the card which would have shown the punctuation of the message was missing, so I have no clue of its meaning, and I have no idea either of how it ended up entombed in the mantel for 75 years.

"At any rate, nothing else happened in the house after that, and we moved out the following November."

And perhaps the resident ghosts were calmed by the odd discovery.

The Exploding Ghost of Andalusia

The setting of this story was an old, abandoned, three-story frame building at what was only described as "The Old Andalusia College"—a ten-minute walk, its protagonists said, from the Pennsylvania Railroad Station.

Details of what set the spirit energy in motion is veiled by time, but it is suspected that the slaying of one "Dr. Chapman" in or near that building led to what two ghost hunters experienced in December, 1884.

According to researchers, Dr. Chapman's wife and a man identified only as "Minor" conspired in 1866 to poison the doctor with arsenic. Minor was later hanged for the crime, but the woman was not punished.

What the lawyer and the cigar-maker experienced was a harrowing night within the walls of a place people in the neighborhood had long held to be haunted.

The story was told by Horace W. Eshback, a lawyer who maintained a practice at 508 Walnut Street. His partner in the spirit search, and the man who would corroborate every word Attorney Eshback would report, was Frank Tygh, a cigar maker who maintained a shop at 6th and Locust Sts.

The men were invited to Andalusia by a friend, John Endicott, who resided in a corner of the old, 20-room building.

47

"We went there about midnight," Eshback told a city newspaper reporter. "We entered a room and thought someone was yelling.

"I told Frank it was only the wind. The wind was really howling as if the imps of iniquity were frenzied in the delights of a free night.

"Suddenly a light spread throughout the room, a light like that produced by a candle.

"In the surprise—or rather, astonishment—of the moment I turned and sat up. I'll tell you that what I saw made me sick and I wished I was almost anywhere else.

"Before me was what appeared to be the bust of a man, perhaps 45 years of age, the shoulders covered with a mantle.

"The face had a perfectly natural appearance, only the lack of mobility. And the head seemed to be resting on a cloud of snow.

"The terrible apparition was moving about the room and I thought it might be a robber. I noticed there were no lower limbs.

"It glided around like a balloon. Now, I am not a believer in spirits, but I was frightened.

" 'What do you want?' I asked, hardly aware of what I was saying.

"Almost simultaneously, the figure noiselessly *exploded*, and seemed to go straight up through a wall!

"The light did not go out for some time, and gradually it died away, leaving us in darkness."

Both men swore every word was true, and whatever had come to call that night was not of this earth.

The Marching Men of Kensington

The files of the Philadelphia Ghost Hunters Alliance (PGHA) are bulging with mysterious tales told to its researchers by city residents of all social, economic, ethnic, and intellectual levels.

Brushes with the supernatural indeed straddle all peoples, in any time and in any place.

The following story is from a woman who lived in the Kensington neighborhood of the city in the 1970s, and whose recollections of an incident there and then remain vivid.

She traded her story for anonymity, fearing her present position in life may be imperiled if certain unenlightened associates discover that, as a child, she came in contact with drumming, marching, and quite *ghostly* men.

"When I was four," the woman began in her written statement, "my mother and I live with my grandfather. My mother, brother and sister lived there as well. Mom and I shared a bedroom.

"From my bed in the middle room I could easily look out into the hall and see the steps. This is where I would see the ghosts.

"Every night like clockwork, or so it seemed, they would come. Their music could be heard first, then came all four men, marching up the stairs. I remember it so clearly. It was very frightening to me.

"Mom was always the first one to fall asleep, leaving me

to lie awake in fear, waiting for our nightly visitors. The music—it was really drumming—always came first. It would start off very low and then gradually got louder as the men got closer to the top of the stairs.

"It wasn't until the drumming reached its peak that the men could be seen, marching up the stairs in single file."

In her mid-30s at the time of publication, the woman still retained a vivid memory of her "marching men."

"All of the men wore a uniform of some sort. As I recall, their jackets were a dark blue. They wore white pants that ended right below the knee, and they wore high socks.

"They seemed to be lit up by some sort of light. They actually had a glow to them.

"They would do the same thing every night, just march and drum. They never looked to their left or right, just straight ahead with emotionless faces, beating on the single drum they each carried."

The midnight muster proved quite frightening for the little girl.

"I would just lay there, stiff as a board from fear, with the blankets pulled up to just below my eyes," she continued.

"As these men reached the top of the steps—the landing—the music would stop. Even though I watched them march up the steps, I never did see them in the hall. They would just disappear!"

And what of the girl's mother, who shared the bed?

"The very first time this happened," our correspondent said, "I tried to wake my mother up. I remember shaking her and at the same time wondering why no one else in the house had heard the drums or seen the men.

"Obviously, they never did."

Now very involved in the quest for more paranormal activity, the woman continues to be perplexed by the marching men of her childhood

"I have tried to come up with an explanation for this all my life," she said, "and never have one.

"I never did sleep in that house until mom and I got a place of our own. Even then it took me a long time to sleep at night.

"I would wake up every night expecting to see the marching men I was all too familiar with. They never came."

For that, she added, she was grateful. And although she is long gone from that old house in Kensington, the place still remains.

"My grandfather hasn't lived in that house for many, many years, either," she continued.

"I sometimes wonder if another little girl lives there now, and if she, too, can see and hear the ghosts that I once did so long ago."

The "Lantern Ghost" of the Moshulu

In the golden age of sail and when the Philadelphia waterfront had few rivals, hundreds of tall masts poked into the sky along the western shore of the Delaware River.

Those days are long gone, but among several historic ships docked on the Delaware these days is the Moshulu (the accent's on the *shu*), arguably the most unusual restaurant in the city.

Diners walk on slightly pitched hardwood decks and duck through low overheads. They peer through hatchways or portholes. In season, they dine on the main weather deck of the vessel.

One may revel in the ship's checkered history—a history that brought the Moshulu from the pinnacle of sailing successes to the pits of seagoing subservience.

The life of the ship is detailed in displays and exhibits

on the upper decks, a film of the 394-foot ship rounding Cape Horn, and in books.

It is the world's largest and oldest four-masted sailing ship still afloat—and some say it is haunted.

The 3,116-ton vessel was launched in Scotland in 1904, and was christened the "Kurt" by her German owners. She plied the seas with general cargoes until World War I when the Americans captured her and renamed her the Moshulu, a Seneca word for "fearless."

Her new owners placed her into the lucrative grain trade, and she quickly gained status as one of the fastest grain-carrying square-riggers on any ocean.

She proved herself in 1939 when she won the Great Grain Race from Australia to England. That race was considered by most maritime historians to be the dying gasp of the square-rigger era.

A fate that awaited many of the majestic sailing ships befell the Moshulu in 1940. Her masts and rigging, her 45,000 square feet of canvas, and her very innards were stripped from her hull and the once-proud Moshulu became a barge—a floating warehouse.

In 1970, the ship was towed to Philadelphia, and after a $2 million renovation, opened as a floating restaurant five years later.

Ill fortune visited the Moshulu once again in the summer of 1989 when a four-alarm fire and smoke damage caused the closing of the restaurant and sent the ship to an uncertain fate at a pier in Camden.

For a while, it seemed as if the veteran of 54 voyages around Cape Horn might wind up in the scrap heap of sailing history.

There were plans proposed that would have kept the Moshulu in Camden, or moved it to Wilmington, Delaware.

Both cities offered millions of dollars in harbor accommodations to the new owners if they would refurbish it and move it to their waterfronts.

But, Philadelphia had the pier, the parking, and Penn's Landing, and the developers, Michael J. Asbell and Eli Karetny, opted to return the Moshulu to Pier 34, where the ship is the centerpiece of a cluster of dining and entertainment facilities.

The Moshulu wears its latest, $11 million renovation with pride. Central American mahogany, Victorian etched glass, bright brasswork, a cocktail lounge, and atmospheric dining rooms on the main deck wrap customers in luxury.

On the upper deck are restored crew's quarters, the galley, the foc'sle, some displays...and one of the invisible crew members.

Eli Karetny, ex-Marine and affable "captain" of the Moshulu, has no trouble speaking of the ghost of the big ship.

"*Ghosts*, that is," he is quick to correct.

It seems that Karetny, and several folks who work aboard the Moshulu, believe there are actually two spirits who stroll the decks of the ship.

An independent investigation of the alleged Moshulu haunting actually turned up what could be a *third* ghost. More on that later.

"We have lanterns on each of the 52 dining tables," Karetny explained. "We do not light those lanterns during the day," he continued.

"But someone does!

"At night, after we have definitely blown out every

single candle–and we double check to make sure we have–some of them relight."

Karetny calmly recalled several occasions when the lantern candles, which had absolutely been snuffed, were found flickering in the light of day.

"At first, we thought we were just seeing bright sunshine coming through the glass of the lanterns," he said. "We checked, and no, it was a flame in the lantern."

The logical culprits might have been the overnight cleaning crew.

"No," Karetny said, "they were not pulling tricks. In fact, they have seen the lanterns light. They were convinced that something unreal was going on. They heard sounds, they saw the lanterns lit up."

In fact, that crew, which worked from midnight to 5 a.m., asked for earlier hours when others are on board. "They were spooked," Karetny quipped.

Patrick Wall, who has tended bar in the ship's Wintergarden Lounge since it reopened, confirmed the strange relighting of candles, as did several other employees.

"All the servers have witnessed it," Karetny continued. "We've come to call it the 'Lantern Ghost'".

The second spirit wanders the upper deck, among the masts and superstructures.

"That ghost," Karetny said, "is probably a sea captain or sailor.

"Day or night you will hear it. You'll hear the sound a lot in the early evening, or right before we close. Guests have heard it.

"It'll be light words, unintelligible. They seem to be coming from the rigging. You have to remember that this ship went around Cape Horn 54 times and 28 men lost their lives. We truly believe the spirits of those lost on those voyages remain on these decks."

But, of course, it is an old, floating, square-rigger. Can its peculiar sounds tease the imagination into believing that a natural creaking of timbers is an unnatural, ghostly soliloquy?

Karetny knows better.

"There are what I call 'mistaken ghosts,' too," he is quick to add.

"This ship talks. Since we're moored here to Pier 34, the ship pulls on its mooring when the tide changes. It's best at night, when it's dark...very mysterious and very wonderful.

"It's as if the ship is tugging and talking, and telling us somehow that it wants to go out, once again, to sea."

Hostess Nina Pasquini confirmed that she and others have heard the voices, and not the "mistaken ghosts."

And restaurant crew member Gary Goldstein said he once heard the sound of a laughing woman on board, long after all guests had gone ashore.

"I asked my manager if he heard it," Goldstein said. "He said it was just the wind in the rigging. I knew it wasn't. It was a woman laughing hysterically, and I know what a woman's laughter sounds like.

"It was coming from the ladies' room, so I went over there and opened the door. As soon as I opened the door, the laughter stopped. But it definitely had been there."

Goldstein may be on to something.

Unbeknownst to Karetny, a medium was dispatched for dinner and a "reading" of the big ship one early evening in early 1998.

She needed only to step onto the gangplank of the

Moshulu to detect its strongest spirit.

"Oh, yes," the paranormal investigator said eagerly, "there's a very strong energy here."

With the full knowledge of the history of the ship and its suspected spiritual inhabitants in hand, the medium shook her head and said the strongest energy was not that of a doomed deckhand and not an old sea captain.

"I don't know exactly when, why, how, or who," she said, "but I suspect the strongest energy is that of a middle-aged woman.

"She might have been the wife of a captain, or a crew member. In fact—and this is just a feeling—I believe she may have been a woman dressed in man's clothing and posing as a male sailor for whatever reason. Or, she could have been a stowaway."

The reader, who preferred we not use her name, felt there were "very odd" circumstances about the woman's time aboard the Moshulu, and even stranger circumstances revolving around her demise.

"I don't feel murder, or suicide," she said. "I do sense confusion and deceit. It's hard to read. There are only bits and pieces of information here. But it's female, very secretive, and very difficult to decipher.

"The energy would be strong enough to spark a candle or recapture conversations. And I think that while it's very bizarre, it's totally harmless."

She added that the nature of the ghost she felt was such that someone with a deep interest in the sea—and especially a *woman* with a deep interest in the sea—would be the most likely to actually see the form of the elusive spirit.

The Spectral Typist
of the Historical Society

No one has seen him. No one fears him. And yet, everyone seems to feel his presence and know his story.

He is the ghost known as "Albert J," and his edifice of eternal existence is no less a prestigious place than the Historical Society of Pennsylvania, 1300 Locust Street.

The society, founded in 1824, is highly regarded amongst scholars for its extensive collection of artifacts which include—but are not limited to—Benjamin Franklin's music stand, Abraham Lincoln's hickory chair, William Penn's family chest, Robert Morris's strongbox, and one of the largest historical libraries of its kind in the United States.

It is the repository for all things Pennsylvanian, and a research facility *par excellence*.

And, they say, it is haunted.

The "they" in this case are any number of past and present employees on all levels of operations at what is one of the first and one of the finest state historical societies in the country.

Among them is Daniel N. Rolph, PhD., reference librarian and collections specialist. A gentleman some might think would have none of any notion that ghosts glide within the walls of such a fine and respected institution.

Au contraire!

You see, Dr. Rolph is a lifelong believer in the mysteries of the supernatural, and has done a fair amount of research on ghosts.

In fact, he earned his doctorate in folklore by writing a book on family stories in his native Kentucky—many of which involved ghosts.

Dr. Rolph came to the HSP in the mid-1980s, and his voice still carries the lilting roll of a Bluegrass brogue.

"When I first came here," he said, "I was told that a former librarian who worked here haunted the place.

"So automatically I was curious, because I grew up hearing family ghost stories down in Kentucky."

Throughout an interview with Dr. Rolph for this book, there was never a hint of skepticism or doubt. He believes.

"The story was that Albert J. Edmunds, who was a cataloger here for 40-odd years, is the ghost.

"According to tradition, he claimed he would work here until he died here, and come back to haunt the place!"

Later research revealed that Edmunds did not, in fact, die at the HSP, but at his home in the Philadelphia suburbs.

But, according to Dr. Rolph and several other staff members at the society, the spirit they have come to call "Albert J" indeed remains within the walls of the institution.

Edmunds came to the United States from his native England in the 1880s, and brought to his work at the Historical Society a broad background in languages (he was fluent in several), comparative religion, and spiritualism.

"He had actually been involved in a ghost story at a library in England," Dr. Rolph said of Edmunds. "I find it interesting that the individual supposed to be the ghost here was himself interested in spectral research."

A prolific writer, Edmunds was well-respected in Philadelphia scholarly circles, and was a tireless worker who played a major role in the organization of the society's vast collections, now estimated to be close to 15 million items.

Edmunds toiled in a room on the third floor, and it is in that chamber from which the vortex of ghostly energy seems to swirl.

"That room has quite a history," Dr. Rolph said.

Over the years, and up to the present, "Albert J" has made his presence known to caretakers, catalogers, independent researchers, and innocent visitors to the HSP.

"A caretaker who used to live here told a story," Dr. Rolph recalled. "One early morning, before anyone was here, he heard a typewriter pecking away in Albert's former office.

"He thought someone had snuck in. He thought he'd, in turn, sneak up on the culprit.

"He got right to the door itself and was getting ready to put his hands on the door knob and could still hear the typewriter going inside the room.

"As soon as he put his hand on the door knob, it stopped. He hurried, yanked the door open, looked in, and there was nothing."

Dr. Rolph pointed out that the old office—which has since been reconfigured—was quite small, and there was no place for anyone to have hidden.

The room was empty when that caretaker entered, but he stands by his experience.

Daniel Rolph also stands by the man's story, because he, too, has heard the eerie sound of an old, manual typewriter clicking away under a phantom's fingers.

Another person who is confident that "Albert J" may still be typing away in his old office is John Platt, who was head librarian and cataloger at the HSP from 1958 until 1982, when he became the executive director of the Masonic Library and Museum of Pennsylvania on North Broad Street.

Platt remembered several episodes in and around Edmunds' old third floor office.

"That room was many things after 'Albert J' passed on," Platt remembered. It had been, among other things, the staff smoking lounge, and a general workroom

"Many times, particularly at night, you could be walking up there and all of a sudden you would hear the sound of a manual typewriter typing away like mad. It was always from 'Albert J's' old office on the 13th Street side of the third floor.

"It would be typing away and typing away, but the moment you would open the door to the room, the typing would cease!

"You'd close the door, walk away, and the typing would begin again.

"It wasn't just me, several staff members heard it. It was the craziest thing!"

On other occasions, HSP workers have reported hearing, feeling, and seeing unexplained phenomena in various parts of the building.

"One time," Dr. Rolph continued, "an address-label machine starting kicking out labels in alphabetical order. But, the machine had no label plates in it—and it wasn't even plugged in!

John Platt was one of three witnesses to that odd event.

While no one claims to have ever seen "Albert J" roaming the corridors and chambers of the building, one maintenance worker said she saw fleeting, shadowy forms pass by her–two or three figures she believed were of an otherworldly origin.

A page at the historical society page did report seeing something untoward in the stacks on the fourth floor, but left only a sketchy story before fleeing in fear.

"I could tell he was scared," Dr. Rolph said. "I remember the night. Whatever it was, he was frightened to death. He wouldn't tell us what he saw, but he quit within two weeks or so."

"Another individual who was head of maintenance a few years ago was here with his son on Christmas eve. They were down in the gallery and heard voices coming from the other side of one of the gallery walls," Dr. Rolph said.

"They said they definitely heard two people speaking to each other. There wasn't anyone around, nobody was in the building, and yet they heard those voices.

"They checked the rooms, and found nothing...no one.

"And, another former maintenance person mentioned to me many times that he would hear footsteps on the third floor. One time, after he had positively turned the elevator off for the day, he positively heard it operating on its own!"

Other random stories include employees and researchers hearing books seeming to shuffle themselves in and out of shelves, and having the disconcerting feeling that someone–or something–is peering over their shoulder.

The story of the ghost of "Albert J" is known to all at the Historical Society. Some shun it, some shy from it, and some shiver at the mention.

"I've been the resident ghost hunter, if you will," Dr. Rolph chuckled.

"In fact, in late 1997, we had a staff meeting and what I did was talk about some of the ghostly happenings in the place."

[Author's Note: Ironically, and perhaps by some strange intervention, it was later that day when David J. Seibold, researcher for this story, contacted Dr. Rolph regarding the ghost story of the Historical Society.]

Over the years, Dr. Rolph has had the opportunity to study a bit of what made Albert J. Edmunds a very special man.

Edmunds was a prolific writer and diarist, and Dr. Rolph has examined his work.

"He called the Historical Society 'The Ground Floor of Hell' for some reason. I always thought that was curious.

"So, it doesn't surprise me at all that he is the ghost of this building. Albert was very deeply involved in psychic phenomena."

The Historical Society of Pennsylvania stands on the site of an old mansion in which a man died.

"I was always curious," Dr. Rolph speculated, "if any of the spectral activity here and now might be related or traceable to that individual.

"I am a firm believer in the existence of disembodied spirits, ghosts, and things of that nature. But, I think some times that what we interpret as 'ghosts' are not ghosts at all.

"What we see or hear and call ghostly are in reality people living and making noises within their own time frames.

"In other words, that time is interdimensional, and that

63

many times when you hear stories about ghosts dressed in period costumes, I think possibly we are seeing back into time or hearing back into time, and we see and hear those people in *their* time frames.

"And, the connections just aren't crystal clear, if you will, so they *appear* to be ghost-like or shadowy.

"It's my theory, and it might explain some of this."

Dr. Rolph has spent the better part of his life studying folklore, and ties together what *is* and what *might have been* in his thoughts.

"Not everything is labeled and can be scientifically explained," he said. "There are many things that at one time were considered folklore or superstition that we have now come to know as fact.

"It's what makes life interesting."

Rappers, Rogues, and Witches

When related to things of a supernatural vein, the City of Brotherly Love takes its place among the most intriguing of all cities in America.

From its very beginnings, Philadelphia has been the setting for many bizarre events, people, and places.

From the deep, mysterious gorge of the Wissahickon Creek to the banks of the Schuylkill and Delaware rivers—from the flatlands of South Philadelphia to the highlands of Chestnut Hill and Mount Airy, virtually every neighborhood has its tales and characters.

Some linger as wisps of legends, while others remain indelible imprints in the annals of Philadelphia history.

Some seem to defy the imagination. Others tease and tempt it.

And although Philadelphia is not situated on an exotic island, it has its pirate stories.

Although it is not Salem, Massachusetts, it has its tales of witches.

And although it's not Lily Dale, New York, it has its stories of rappers and spiritualists.

There are vague and vaporous references in Philadelphia history to odd cults, such as the "Millerites."

In 1843, a preacher named Harman Osler attempted to ignite the citizenry to unite and face the end of the world, which Osler claimed would occur on October 23, 1844.

A handful of folks elected to follow his urgings, and those who did fashioned "ascension robes" which would be worn on the appointed day for the appointment with destiny.

That day came...and went...and the world, as well as the Millerites, somehow survived.

Nudists, Thugs, and Buccaneers

And then there were the "Rogerines," who raised some eyebrows (and, no doubt, some eye *lids*) in the early 18th century when they carried on their society *in the nude* on the banks of the Delaware River.

Little more than that is known about this peculiar sect.

That very same Delaware waterfront has been a breeding ground for malcontents and miscreants for literally hundreds of years.

Anyone who grew up in Philadelphia in the late 20th century will recall with disdain the scourge of gangs and hoodlums who terrorized and disgraced entire neighborhoods with graffiti, turf wars, and random acts of violence.

There is some solace in the fact that in the mid-*19th* century, Philadelphia was also nearly overrun by loosely-organized gangs.

An 1840s gang with one of the most ominous names was the "Killers," who staked a territorial claim along the waterfront, where their variety of violence was often referred to as "piracy."

Any such dastardly derring-do along the Delaware couldn't hold a candle to other less documented acts of piracy supposed to have played out on the river banks.

An account in a 19th century newspaper article about legends in the city linked one of the most barbarous buccaneers of all time with Philadelphia.

"We can better understand the nightly visitations of spirits whose mortal existence was spent in deeds of violence and crime, and who, like the Ancient Mariner were cursed with the horrible curse of dead men's eyes," the anonymous writer said.

"They," he or she continued, "the pariahs of ghostland, deserve to be fugitives and vagabonds—the fate of all outcasts.

"It is but just that Captain Kidd and his followers who, during their lives, struck terror in the hearts of peaceful citizens, should be doomed as spirits to a perpetual pilgrimage.

"Water Street was for many years, and for all we know, it may be still, their promenading grounds in Philadelphia.

"Booted and sworded, the black flag borne aloft, they march noiselessly through the narrow passageway between the tall houses 'up Walnut and down Front.' until the morning sounds warn them it is time to disappear."

Heavy stuff, indeed!

Pirates were big news when they were active on the river, bay, and shorelines of the region.

And, their stories continued to thrill readers for decades beyond their short but turbulent times.

Old diaries and newspaper clippings tell stories of shipwrecks being pillaged by pirates within sight of Philadelphia's streets, and of the watergoing wastrels who were caught suffering ghastly fates just a stone's throw from the foot of South Street.

One of those who did not escape the law was the Scot pirate known as Wilkinson, who murdered a man in Marcus

Hook, killed three more off Wilmington, and was finally caught in a brutal battle near what is now the Pennsylvania/Delaware border along the Delaware River. While Wilkinson was taken into custody, a dozen of his cutthroats were gunned down.

Wilkinson was imprisoned in the Walnut Street Prison, and after a daring escape attempt, was finally hanged.

An article in the Philadelphia *Times* in 1897 graphically illustrated the fate of Wilkinson and his ilk:

"How gruesome it must have been about 1780," the article noted, "when the bones of the Tory and Privateer Wilkinson hung from a post on the sands about opposite South Street, swinging and creaking in the blast through the long, winter night."

Treasure Hunters Beware!

The early German settlers called their spirits "schpuks," from which we get our word "spook."

One account from an old folklore study corroborated the pirates' tales, and added another ne'er-do-well to the mix.

"An idea was very prevalent," the writer said, "that the pirates of Black Beard's day had deposited treasure in the earth.

"The fancy was that sometimes they killed a prisoner and interred him with it, to make his ghost keep his vigils there and guard it.

"Hence, it was not rare to hear of persons having seen a 'schpuk' or ghost, which became a strong incentive to dig there."

"Hexers," or conjurors, would be consulted by some treasure-seekers, and many a night in early Philadelphia would pass with several fortune hunters digging in the muddy soil of the Schuylkill and Delaware river banks in hopes of finding a buried treasure and not drawing the wrath of a pirate's ghost.

The practice became so laughable to more practical citizens that skits and plays were written and presented in ridicule of these midnight excavations.

One such account remains in the library of the Athenaeum, in which the lead character exclaims to his wife, in a mocking dialect: "My dearest wife, in all my life...Ich neber was so frightened. De spirit come, und ich did run...'twas just like tunder, mit lightning!"

In their book, "Rebels and Gentlemen," authors Carl and Jessica Bridenbaugh noted that in 1767, Col. Thomas Forrest wrote a play which, in the Bridenbaughs' words, "joyfully satirized the foibles of a credulous group of middle- and lower-class Philadelphians who had embarked on an absurd get-rich-quick scheme for recovering the hidden pirate treasures of Kidd and Blackbeard."

"This foolish passion for 'digging,'" they continued, was an old one, toward which as early as 1729 Franklin had directed in one of his little essays."

The play was never actually presented.

Col. Forrest, known in society circles as quite the practical joker, was known to set up groups of unsuspecting friends with ghastly and elaborate charades in which the group would "conjure up" spirits who would lead them to buried treasure, sometimes as far away as the New Jersey shore.

All the while, the "ghosts" and the treasure maps were the concoction of Col. Forrest.

Early historical dissertations indicate there may have really been places in Philadelphia at which the booty of pirates and thieves may have been buried.

In John F. Watson's *Annals of Philadelphia*, which was published in 1844, the author noted:

"Several aged persons have occasionally pointed out to me the places where persons, to their knowledge, had dug for pirates' money.

"The small hill once on the north side of Coates Street, near to Front Street, was well remembered by John Brown as having been much dug.

"T. Matlack Esq. told me he was once shown an oak tree at the south end of Front Street, which was marked KLP, at the foot of which was found a large sum of money.

"I heard somewhere that about forty-five years ago, at the Sign of the Cock in Spruce Street, there was found in a pot in the cellar a sum of money of about $5,000.

"In digging in the cellar of the old house at the northeast corner of Second Street and Gray's Alley, they discovered a pot of money there; also some lately at Frankford Creek."

Watson also documented the presence of a black man who lived on the south side of Race Street, a few doors east of Second, and "was stated to have sold himself to the devil."

Hundreds of people visited the man, who was believed to have supernatural powers to heal and to exorcise evil spirits.

A Philadelphia Witch Hunt

In those years when Philadelphia was growing from a "green country town" to a thriving capital city, its citizenry—a curious mix of Quaker and Quirky, lived under some stringent

70

laws.

If they worked on a Sunday, they faced a twenty-shillings fine. If they smoked on a street–twelve pence; if they cursed in public–ten shillings.

And, of course, even the slightest suspicion of any practice of the "black arts" or sorcery would be cause for the most harsh of all punishments, hanging.

Throughout the stacks of Philadelphia history books there are veiled and vague references to individuals who may have drawn such suspicions.

A 1924 book, "A Guide Book of Art, Architecture, and Historic Interests in Pennsylvania," covered its title topics quite thoroughly and quite systematically.

But in a description of the Wissahickon Creek Valley, mention was made of the statue of William Penn which stands upon "Mom Rinker's Rock."

"She," the text reads, "is said to have been a witch."

Who she was and who said she was a witch has been lost in time. A more complete and compelling story about witchcraft in Philadelphia can be found in the very first volume of the Colonial Records of Pennsylvania.

It is the story of Margaret Mattson, the wife of Neels Mattson, the owner of a plantation in Delaware County.

Folks out there called Margaret "The Witch of Ridley Creek." The embryonic Colonial justice system called her a criminal.

It was 1683, and the Provincial Council sat as the court, since a formal court had not yet been organized.

Convening in Philadelphia, the council comprised of prominent lawyers, influential citizens, commonfolk, and a chairman no less powerful than himself, William Penn.

• PHILADELPHIA GHOST STORIES •

In the minutes of Provincial Council, the charge was delineated:

> Henry Drystreet attested, saith he was told 20 years agoe, that the prisoner at the bar was a Witch & that several Cows were bewitched by her; also, that James Saunderling's mother told him that she bewitched her cow, but afterwards said it was a mistake, and that her Cow should doe well againe, for it was not her Cow but an Other Person's that should die.

The accusations mounted as more witnesses offered their testimonies. Farmer Charles Ashcom was one:

> One night the Daughter of ye Prisoner called hastily, and when he came she sayd there was a great Light but Just before, and an Old woman with a Knife in her hand at ye Bedd's feet, and therefore she cried out and desired Jno. Symcock to take away his Calves, or Else she would send them to Hell.

As convoluted as those ancient phrases and spellings may be, they pointed at the time to the belief by several of Margaret Mattson's neighbors that she was possessed.

What the Swedish immigrant was *not* possessed of was the ability to speak and understand English. And, since William Penn knew no Swedish, an individual named Lasse Cock acted as interpreter.

Mattson (whose name has also been recorded as

"Mattison" and "Matson") vehemently denied the accusations:

The Prisoner denyeth all things, and saith that yᵉ Witnesses speake only by hear say.

The council jury deliberated, and rendered an odd verdict:

The Jury went forth, and upon their Returne Brought her in Guilty of haueing the Comon fame of a witch, but not guilty in manner and forme as Shee stand Indicted.

But, there was a punishment doled out:

Neels Mattson and Antho. Neelson Enters into a Recognizance of fifty pounds apiece, for the good behavior of Margaret Mattson for six months.

The first, and the only witchcraft trial in Pennsylvania history was thus concluded.

A Deal with the Devil

Early Colonial records reveal punishments doled out to convicted petty pirates of the Delaware, to blasphemers, and to thugs of all ilk. The stocks and whipping posts were seldom without company.

The diary of Rev. Andreas Sandel included the following entry of January 12, 1716:

A dreadful thing happened in Philadelphia, to the wife of a butcher, who had quarreled with her husband. He asked her to make their bed, but she refused. Continuing to refuse, he told her he would turn her out of the house, but she told him if he did so, she would break every window pane, and invoked the Devil to come for her if she did not do it.

The husband led her out of the house, she became highly excited, broke some of the panes, and through the kitchen made her go up to the attic with a candle, and laid down on the bed greatly disturbed on account of her promise.

Then, she heard somebody coming up the stairs, but saw no one—this was repeated for half an hour. Becoming more and more agitated, fearing her awful invocation was about to be realized, she went down to her husband, telling him of her anguish and asking him to aid her.

Laying down on a bench near the hearth she perceived a dark human face, making horrid grimaces with mouth wide open and the teeth gnashing. Then she became thoroughly terrified and asked her husband to read to her Psalm XXI, which he did, and the face disappeared.

Soon afterwards she perceived at the window, one of which she had broken, that some one was standing there with both arms extended through the window, by which her fright was made greater.

Then, the figure approached and passed her. . .Her

74

husband then clasped his arms around her, when the fumes of brimstone became so strong they could not remain indoors.

At one o'clock she sent for the minister, who also came and prayed with her the next day. Many persons visited her, but she had to hold her hands over her knees to keep from trembling.

The Hermits of the Wissahickon

The earliest records of the Monthly Meeting of Friends revealed the presence of what the Quakers called "black arts."

These "arts" included geomancy, necromancy, and astrology.

Suspected astrologers were soundly condemned and brought before their peers for punishment.

One particular group and several prominent individuals, however, defied their critics and cast new light onto the so-called "black arts."

They have gone down in history—albeit not mainstream history—as the "Hermits of the Wissahickon."

They were called "Pietists," "Mystics," "Diviners," and, yes, "Conjurors."

And despite these descriptions, bordering on what would seem to have been dangerous turf according to early tolerances, these "Hermits" were treated with a certain level of respect.

It is generally regarded that the first Pietists—men influenced by a sect in Frankfurt, Germany, which broke away from the Lutheran faith and incorporated several beliefs and practices (including those of the Quakers and the Mennonites) settled in Germantown in the summer of 1694.

Their earliest leader was Heinrich Bernhard Köster, who drew the curious and some converts.

A schism developed within the ranks of the Pietists, and an extremist named Johannes Kelpius emerged to become the leader.

A Transylvanian transplant, Kelpius and a handful of followers elected to follow a more pure doctrine which suggested celibacy, allowed the practice of astrology, and encouraged abstract and experimental science.

Known as "Kelpians," or "The Society of the Woman of the Wilderness," these practitioners also believed the end of the world was near—that when the 17th century ended, so would all of civilization end.

Kelpius placed his faith in the coming of a "woman clothed with the sun, with the moon under her feet, and the twelve stars on her forehead—she who fled into the wilderness" who would lead the faithful few to glory beyond the Millennium.

It is believed that 14 men chose to live under the most extreme dictums set forth by Kelpius. These 14 were the "Hermits of the Wissahickon."

They lived in caves near springs along the creek, near where a roadbed called "Hermit Lane" courses today.

The last of the hermits were said to have left their stark compound in about 1750.

Kelpius died at about age 35, and tradition has it that among his legacies was the very name of a Philadelphia neighborhood.

Kelpius called his hut "The Burrow of Rocks," as foxes

The "Devil's Pool" in the Wissahickon Creek Gorge, ca. 1910.

often burrowed in the rocky cellar of the place. That name was later formalized to "Rocks Burrow," or as it is now known, "Roxborough."

Tales of "Spook Hill"

From these "Kelpians" emerged one particular man—in fact, the man considered to be the last survivor of the sect—Dr. Christopher Witt.

Also known as "DeWitt," the English doctor embraced the Pietist beliefs in about 1704. Obviously, their prediction of the "end of the world" did not come true.

Dr. Witt, as we shall call him, resided at Germantown Avenue and High Street, and lived there until 1765, when he died at age 90.

Called a mystic by some, a magician by others, and a "spook" by still others, Witt left an indelible mark on the history of Germantown, Philadelphia, and in some ways, the United States.

Witt could be considered a kind of "Renaissance Man" in that he was a physician, a philosopher, a craftsman, an astronomer, and a magician.

Witt planted a sprawling garden of exotic plants and flowers on his property, and when he was not tending what some consider to be the the first botanical garden in the country (predating John Bartram's by two decades), he crafted intricate wall clocks in his workshop.

He built telescopes, a pipe organ, and was regarded generally as a good citizen and honest man.

But, Dr. Witt left behind several legends, and, as if you haven't already guessed, an interesting ghost story.

In those earliest days of Germantown (did you know the town was almost named "Germanopolis" and that it was considered as a site for the capital of the United States?), the kindly Dr. Witt may well have practiced a form of faith healing known in the Pennsylvania German region as "pow-wowing."

To some less tolerant folks, his "healing" powers were translated as "hexing" or "witching" powers. Some believed he was engaged in activity of the "schpuk" variety.

Dr. Witt (and, consider the times here) also kept a slave. History records that man's name as Robert Claymer, and that he was a mulatto of light skin and contemplative demeanor.

Interestingly, in Dr. Witt's will, Robert Claymer was left a "certain tract of land in Germantown on the north side of Keyser's Lane" and all of the doctor's tools and household goods.

Some people who feared and misunderstood Robert spread a vicious rumor that he was not mortal at all, but a "schpuk" summoned up from the grave by Dr. Witt.

In his last years, Dr. Witt's eyesight had failed him, and Robert would lead him through his property and the neighborhood.

Dr. Christopher Witt died in early February, 1765, and was buried in the Warner Graveyard, on High Street in Germantown. The Warner family plot was owned by Christian Warner Sr., one of Dr. Witt's closest friends, to whom he willed all the property which wasn't left to Robert.

Even before his death and burial there, the graveyard on Warner Hill was also known in the town as "Mount Misery" or "Spook Hill."

It was believed by many that at midnight, ghosts strolled between the tombstones. Some even said Dr. Witt and Robert would sneak by lantern-light in the old burial ground and meet with the souls of long-departed comrades.

The night of Dr. Witt's burial, certain neighbors claimed they saw a blue glow swirl around his fresh grave. They said Robert made nightly pilgrimages to the grave. They believed that he communicated with his dead master and friend.

Dr. Witt's spirit is not the only one believed to "reside" at the old Warner Graveyard.

Following the Battle of Germantown, scores of Hessian mercenaries and British soldiers killed in the battle were hastily interred in the cemetery.

That fueled the legend that when all conditions are right—conditions never fully explained by neighbors who claimed to have witnessed the event—the ghost of a British officer, sitting proudly on a gleaming white horse, would silently and slowly ride among the grave markers.

The last burial at the Warner Graveyard was in 1793, and in 1819, St. Michael's Episcopal Church was built on its site.

Katie King Comes to Call

Earlier in this chapter, the town of Lily Dale, New York, was mentioned.

For those not familiar with the village of about 167 acres and 250 permanent residents, it is north of Jamestown and near Interstate 90.

It is a village founded in 1879 by Spiritualists, and an offshoot of those first settlers, the Lily Dale Assembly, owns the entire village.

Things are a bit eerie in the town near the shores of Lake Erie.

The Spiritualism movement was fashioned in the mid-

• PHILADELPHIA GHOST STORIES •

19th century after Margaret and Kate Fox told anyone who would listen that they were able to communicate with the dead through rapping sounds in their tiny cottage in Hydesville, N.Y.

The Fox twins' home was actually moved to Lily Dale after their deaths and was a Mecca of sorts for Spiritualists until it was destroyed by fire in 1955.

Over the years, many notables have come to see what the town of mediums, psychics, and seers had to offer them. Conferences which focused on angels, past life regression, paranormal research, and ghosts have drawn tens of thousands of participants to Lily Dale.

Historically, Spiritualism hit its stride in the 1870s, and Philadelphians felt its impact.

One of the most remarkable cases involved a ghost named Katie King.

For this story, we reference a no less prestigious source than a July 21, 1874 story in *The New York Times*.

Dateline, Philadelphia: Headline: "A Ghost or a Fraud?" Author: An anonymous (and, as you will read, quite opinionated) *Times* correspondent.

Philadelphia was hot copy in July, 1874. The Charlie Ross kidnapping case was making national news (a fascinating case with no supernatural overtones), and a spectacular materialization séance was fueling the fires of Spiritualism.

"Katie King" had made worldwide news earlier in the year when she was conjured up by Florence Cook, a teenage medium, in London. The manifestation of the ghost of Miss King, and scientific investigations which attempted—and failed—to debunk it, had caused quite a stir.

The *Times* writer, who shamefully was never identified,

described Katie as "one part Spiritualism and two parts humbug." But in later paragraphs, his or her thoughts became even more uncompromising.

Nonetheless, the correspondent did acknowledge that Spiritualism, and Katie King had a "noble army of followers, numbering several hundreds in Philadelphia."

There were some rather questionable facets to the Katie King story. She claimed she was the daughter of John King, who as a pirate scourge of the Caribbean went by the name of "Henry Morgan." Her name in life was Annie Morgan, but in the spirit world, Henry was John and Annie was Katie.

Questionable, at best.

But putting any questions aside, the faithful flocked to wherever whomever would call upon their psychic powers to bring Katie King's apparition to the fore.

Such was the case on July 20, 1874, when the *Times* reporter was invited to a comfortable apartment in an old, three-story, brick building at 50 N. 9th Street in Philadelphia.

In a room above a music store—a room in the residence belonging to a couple identified as Mr. and Mrs. Nelson Holmes, several Spiritualists gathered (at a dollar apiece) to witness the ethereal entrance of Katie King.

With a red shade over the coal-oil lamp casting an eerie glow, the Holmes' led the participants in the summoning of the spirit from a large "cabinet" from which she would emerge.

The "cabinet" was standard equipment for the séances of the Spiritualists.

The tall device, in which a living person could easily hide and emerge as the "ghost," could be cause for suspicion.

But in the 9th Street case, and others before, independent skeptics had searched the cabinets for any possible openings through which a mortal might squeeze, and found none.

The newspaper reporter admitted that the cabinet, and in fact, the room in which the séance took place, were literally "torn apart" by cynical professors from the University of Pennsylvania, and nothing untoward had been discovered.

"Naturally," the journalist told the readers, "you will ask for the solution of the mystery. I have none to give. There are, or seems to be, a solid floor beneath, a solid ceiling above, a solid wall on one side, and a solidly-closed door on the other.

"One would think that no mortal could disappear as readily as Katie King does, without being seen by some of the audience, gazing, as they do, point blank through the open door [of the cabinet]."

And what of "the mystery" as described by the writer?

After several minutes of minor-key chanting by the attendees, a window in the cabinet opened, and the chants fell into a hushed silence.

As everyone looked on, wide-eyed and breathless, a pale arm pushed out through the window. And then, a shoulder, and then...the face of the ghost.

Described by the reporter as having a pretty face, a full and round figure, and a "complexion so clear and transparent that it either seemed to, or actually did, shine with a mild radiance," Katie King emerged to muffled gasps.

"There was," the correspondent continued, "a profound silence until she says in a ghostly whisper....'*Good Evening*.'"

Dressed in muslin, her hair in black ringlets, and her

face framed by a Spanish veil, Katie answered simple, salutatory questions, and seemed to materialize and fade as the astonished gathering watched in breathless amazement.

"And then," the *Times* reporter noted, "ensued a brisk dialogue of the smallest kind of small talk, interrupted by frequent disappearances and reappearances on the part of the young lady.

"She came...seeming to gather herself from thin air, and to grow, like a forming cloud, more and more distinct, until she again stood in mortal guide before a delighted audience."

The audience may have been delighted, amazed, and thoroughly convinced that they were watching the emergence of a ghost. But the newspaper person did not share the euphoria.

In the closing lines of his or her lengthy and detailed account of the encounter, the writer made a rather profound conclusion.

If spirits may revisit earth only to talk nonsense, if they can do nothing but prattle and look pretty, and can impart no information of man's state, either present or future, then it seems to me that Spiritualism is a fraud of the biggest kind, and that the spirits would do much better to stay home and let us form for ourselves other views of the hereafter than than which must regard it as simply an asylum for feeble-minded ghosts.

Given the technology and reportage of the late 20th century, whatever transpired in that Ninth Street building in July of 1874 may well have been exposed more quickly for what the newspaper reporter believed it was.

But in that age, so much darker in the understanding of the paranormal and the ability to investigate it, Katie King continued to dazzle a perhaps unsuspecting public.

But not for long.

On October 23, Katie King returned to Philadelphia, where she was contacted by what another reporter called "a gentleman whose name, were I permitted to give it, would be recognized by hundreds of persons in Philadelphia's best society."

In a daylight encounter with the spirit, those in attendance were treated to not only the apparition of Miss King, but a long session of "spirit writing."

But, the Katie King phenomenon began to unravel when a respected "German scientist" in attendance issued his opinion of the "spirit."

"Katie King," he told those in the room, "is a bad young woman who goes about the country in the company of her mother, making money out of the credulity of those who are foolish enough to pay to see her perform her tricks. There is no mistake about it. She is simply and purely a humbug, as are most professional mediums."

Two months later, stories spread across the pages of newspapers across America that a Philadelphia *Inquirer* investigation had indeed discovered that Katie King was not a ghost at all.

She was, the newspaper said, a "fraud," and was a widow with a child—basically a "street person" who, with the encouragement of her mother and hosts such as the Holmes', devised the money-making scheme.

"The trick of the mediums," the article said, "has been exposed, and the personator of the departed Katie King has confessed her share in the imposture, and has returned the gifts which she received from the credulous people who thought she had taken them into the spirit world with her."

British writer and researcher of the occult Lewis Spence, in his authoritative *The Encyclopædia of the Occult*, stated, "There is no doubt that fraud entered, and still enters, very largely into materialisation séances...skepticism is not altogether unjustified."

But Spence did not totally rule out the possibility that other types of séances, and the spirits conjured up in them may have been, and may still be, quite authentic.

The Screaming Lady, the Faceless Man, and other Phantoms of Old Fort Mifflin

In the autumn of 1777, a beleaguered Colonial garrison at a muddy, mesquito-infested fort south of Philadelphia fought valiantly (and ultimately in vain) to save a bastion of defense against British invaders.

Two centuries later, the fort lay in near ruins. Thoughtless "campers" accidentally started a fire that consumed the two-story commandant's residence in the middle of the fort parade ground. Thick vines, flood sludge, and underbrush crawled over, around, and through the walls of the fort.

What could not be done by British cannonballs was being achieved by the irrepressible forces of nature. An important historic shrine was under attack and losing the battle.

But in 1989, after an energetic fund- and awareness-raising appeal, Old Fort Mifflin was rescued, refurbished, and reopened to a public that had all but forgotten it.

So where was the fort all those decades? Actually, it has always been one of the most visible historic sites in the city. Thousands of people could see it every day, if they chose to. Fort Mifflin was right under their noses.

It is actually right under the noses of the hundreds of

Ghostly sounds and apparitions have been noticed in and around the ruins of the Commandant's House at Old Fort Mifflin.

airplanes that take off and touch down every day at Philadelphia International Airport.

For those who have flown into the airport, Fort Mifflin is the star-shaped structure that is just under the belly of the plane as it coasts onto the runway.

Now operated by a non-profit corporation, Old Fort Mifflin is growing as a tourist attraction and a place where students may have a close look at a Revolutionary War fort

Of all the programs and special events held in the busy calendar of the fort, its Halloween ghost tours have taken their place among the most popular.

And for very good reasons: The Old Lamplighter...the Blacksmith...the Screaming Lady...and the Man with No Face.

Ghosts, one and all.

Throughout the many months and many miles spent researching this book, the research team and author have come up against innumerable intransigents who have acknowledged the legends, stories, and even personal experiences of their particular places, but have refused to allow the tales to be retold in this volume.

Some reasons seemed valid, but most seemed vapid.

Twas not the case at Old Fort Mifflin, where Executive Director Dori McMunn was pleased to introduce us to the many manifestations who roam the 14 buildings and 50 acres of the underappreciated attraction.

"We've all had things happen—staff and visitors alike," the effervescent Drexel Hill native said in her crowded office on the second floor of the 1829-era hospital building, which was restored in 1988.

As we discussed the phantoms of the fort, Patriot, the cat whom Dori calls "our environmentally-correct mouse control unit," dozed on a cozy comforter.

Ms. McMunn owes her interest in history to her father, who took his young daughter to virtually every historical site in the region. For that, she is grateful.

She owes her understanding of the supernatural to the site she became commander-in-chief of in the early 1990s.

"I can't say I really bought into any of that ghost stuff until I'd been here a little while. I'd never had any experiences with it," she said.

That all changed, and in short order.

The stories about the ghosts at the fort had been circulating for decades.

There are marquee and mundane ghost there, and Dori McMunn says the stars of the supernatural show depend on "where you are and what you do here."

"If you're a visitor, the hallmark person seems to be the screaming woman of the officers quarters. Often, little children have seen her and ask us who the woman in the window is."

Thing is....there *is* no woman in the window. No mortal woman, at least!

"If you work in this office, the old hospital building," she continued, "it's 'Edward.' Edward is very ill, and he's apparently in a cot in the room adjacent to my office."

Dori proceeded to reel off several odd incidents which have been attributed to Edward.

"We can't open doors sometimes, drawers open and close on their own, things like that. After a while, and I hate to say this, we've all become somewhat desensitized to it."

Dori said the screaming woman and Edward are not the only spirits said to roam the fort's grounds.

"A third important spirit here is Jacob, the blacksmith," she said.

"And, there are more ghosts....many more," she added.

Before we meet those ghosts, a little background on the bastion at the end of the runway—a fort which could well be called the "Alamo along the Delaware."

It was British army engineer John Montresor who designed the original fortification on Mud Island, which was out about 500 feet from the Pennsylvania mainland.

In 1772, construction of a stone-walled fort began on the island, but within a year the British felt the strong rumblings of the embryonic struggle for independence. The building of the fort was abruptly halted.

By 1776, those rumblings exploded into revolution, and a committee chaired by—who else?—Benjamin Franklin—organized strategic defenses for Philadelphia.

Fort Mercer was built on the New Jersey side and the unfinished British fortifications on Mud Island were shored up and completed under the direction of Maj. Gen. Thomas Mifflin, who would later become the first governor of Pennsylvania.

The original fort was a crude collection of earth and timber, but it served the purpose.

In autumn, 1777, Sir William Howe's Redcoats were celebrating victory upon victory, and Howe devised a plan to send a massive flotilla of British warships up the Delaware bay and river and into Philadelphia to gain needed supplies.

Howe mocked the defenses set up at the entrance to the port. Battles ensued along both shores of the river, and somehow the Colonial defenders hung tough despite the thousands of Hessian and British forces who pounded their positions on all fronts.

On the New Jersey side, 400 Colonials beat back the British. From the Pennsylvania shore, booming cannons blew up the massive, 64-gun battlewagon HMS Augusta as it was mired helplessly in the mud of the river.

It was said the final explosion of the Augusta was heard as far away as Reading.

The British pressed on and threw all they had into the fray. On November 10, the cannons roared and Fort Mifflin was alternately destroyed and rebuilt as the garrison somehow withstood the assault.

The death blow for Fort Mifflin came November 15, 1777, when British troops on land and sea overran and set fire to the fort as the handful of Colonial survivors fled in the dark of the night. An estimated 70 percent of the garrison had become casualties.

But damage had also been done to the British plans. Gen. Washington had organized and established his army at Valley Forge, winter had limited any British troop movements, and the action along the Delaware had given the Colonial army time to rest and strategize.

The installation on Mud Island was rebuilt in 1795, and through the War of 1812, the Civil War, and as recently as the Korean War, Fort Mifflin remained a cog in the gears of American defense.

Confederate prisoners were confined and there were executions within its walls during the Civil War, and during the 20th century, ammunition and other supplies were stored there.

Fort Mifflin was finally decommissioned in 1962 and turned over to the city of Philadelphia. Under Mayor Edward

Rendell's "privatization" plan which turned several city-owned historical attractions to non-profit organizational hands, the fort became self-governing.

Enough history. Now, let us greet those phantoms of Fort Mifflin.

They are truly all around, everywhere inside the fort. One can scarcely walk 15 feet without setting foot into the realm of a wraith.

Your author and Ms. McMunn walked from the hospital/office building, as a cold winter rain sprayed us and giant jets roared their way into and out of the nearby airport.

As we crossed over the moat and through the North Sallyport, now the visitors entrance, two buildings flanked us. The storehouse to the left now houses modernized facilities, but the Soldiers' Barracks to the right has been restored to look as it might have when some 250 enlisted men bunked there.

It is on the porticoes of the Soldiers' Barracks that the ghost of the fort's lamplighter maintains its vigil.

"A couple people have bumped into him," Dori said. "We always thought it was a joke until we ran into documentation that we did indeed have oil lamps that needed to be lit at twilight."

A medium who toured the fort declared that the lamplighter's name was John—perhaps John Adkins or Akins—and his ghost can be seen usually walking the second floor porch of the barracks.

It was near the staircase to that second level, Ms. McMunn noted, that a fort volunteer once watched in amazement as the fort's two German Shepherd guard dogs once cowered, their hair standing on end, barking at an unseen intruder.

But, that "unseen" lamplighter has actually been seen by unaware visitors not predisposed to any knowledge of his presence.

More than one tourist has reported seeing or feeling either the lamplighter, or the softly-glowing lamps he once lit, and perhaps still does light.

In the middle of the fort are the eerie ruins of the Commandant's House. Burned in a 1980 accident, it stands in the middle of the Parade Grounds, upon which the ghosts of both Confederate and Union soldiers still march and camp, in their time at that place.

From the Commandant's House has been heard the ethereal echo of bells, presumably from a bell tower which stood on its roof. Weeping sounds have been heard near its walls.

"But, I guess the most colorful ghost here," Dori McMunn said, "is the 'screaming woman.'"

"A lot of people have experienced her."

From psychics and mediums to school children and their mentors, and to the caretaker of the fort, dozens of folks have casually asked about the woman whose face has been seen in, and whose moaning and screaming has been heard from the second level of the Officers' Quarters.

Built in 1814 on the site of the 1776-era Soldiers Barracks which were destroyed in the 1777 assault, the Officers' Quarters holds within its walls many stories, to be sure.

"One time," the executive director noted, "a bunch of ten-year old girls were here for a tour. We went into the Soldiers' Barracks and I was doing my spiel when one of the girls asked who was the lady in the window.

"She was pointing over to the Officers' Quarters, and she insisted she had seen the face of a lady in the window on the second floor."

Dori tried to sluff off the girl's claim, but the student was adamant.

"She wasn't the first kid to see her," she said, "but I didn't tell her about the 'screaming woman' ghost because they were here for a tour, and I didn't want to create a stir."

It is believed that the "Screaming Woman" is Elizabeth Pratt, who will appear in Revolutionary War garb and is liable to burst into frantic sobbing at any time.

They say Elizabeth mourns the death of her daughter–a daughter who had been estranged from the family and died of dysentery in about 1801. The mother wails because she never made amends with her daughter before she passed away. Elizabeth supposedly committed suicide a year after her daughter's death.

So vivid has the screaming sound been that on one occasion, the Philadelphia police were actually called to the fort because someone believed a woman was in trouble somewhere on the grounds. A thorough check was made, and nothing, at least nothing of this life and this earth, was found.

Another spirit which has been reported by several people on several occasions is that of a chap named Jacob Sauer.

Jacob was the civilian blacksmith in the fort, sometime around the Civil War.

His ghost has been heard clunking away in the Blacksmith Shop, which was restored in 1969, and has been seen standing in front of the door to the shop, which often creaks open or slams shut, supposedly by Jacob's gentle hand.

Near the Artillery Shed at the rear of the fort, the ghost of a Civil War captain still inspects his arsenal, and just to the east end of the shed, the lonely ghost of a young Revolutionary War foot soldier named Amos sits confused, cleaning his gun, awaiting further orders.

As the tour guides at Fort Mifflin are sensitive to young minds' interpretation of these apparitions, Dori said they are also sensitive to even the adults' thinking when the notion of another very prominent spirit is pondered.

The fort personnel hesitate telling the story of what could be called the "Ghostly Guide" for fear that the tale could spook anyone, at any age, and spoil what should be an enjoyable visit.

"One day we were having an event on the parade grounds," Ms. McMunn explained. "Everyone was in Revolutionary War uniforms.

"A woman came up to me praising, absolutely *praising*, a man who led a tour through what we call the 'dungeons.' I thanked her. She was just gushing about the tour guide. She said he gave her more information than she ever could have imagined."

It was, she said, as if that guide had lived the life of a soldier at Fort Mifflin.

Perhaps he had!

"I asked her to tell me what he looked like, so I could commend him. She told me he had a Civil War uniform on. Well, at that, I was taken back.

"You see, there *was no one* on the grounds in a Civil War uniform that day. It was a Revolutionary War

96

The ghost of a faceless man and several unknown ghostly soldiers have been sighted in the "dungeon" Casemates of Old Fort Mifflin.

reenactment day. But she was positive it was a Civil War uniform, and said she knew the difference between the two war uniforms."

It is not unusual for a program at Fort Mifflin to invite and feature either Revolutionary War or Civil War reenactors—living, breathing men and women of the present who dress and act as their counterparts would have so many centuries ago.

And, it is not unusual for these living, breathing, men and women of the present to see, hear, or feel those counterparts of so many centuries ago.

Most of those unearthly interactions have taken place in and around the Casemates which extend under the ramparts on the river side of the fort, near the original Main Gate and the remnants of the original 1776 fort walls—walls which still bear pock marks from British cannonballs.

It is in those Casemates, which served as bombproof shelters and later prison cells, where Melvin, Alexander, Michael, and the "Faceless Man" may be encountered.

Easily the most ominous environs on the grounds of the fort, the "dungeon" are deep, dark, and dank. They are home to the occasional bird who flutters in to scatter the occasional small rodent which may scurry about in the cool catacombs.

At the entrance to the Casemates dwell the spirits of Alexander and Michael, who stand eternal guard. And, in one corner of the stony portal is a mysterious man who sits and sews, and when he looks up at whoever may pass by, there is nothing where his face should be—only a blank, hollow void under a rumpled cloth hat.

He is the "Faceless Man" of the fort.

He may be faceless, but he is not alone in the darkness of eternity.

Mediums claim there are many ghosts in the Casemates—ghosts standing by a fireplace in the largest chamber, ghosts of Confederate soldiers mulling about in the hallway, the ghost of an old Union ordnance sergeant named Bromley, and an unknown ghost which appears as a bluish glow in the impenetrable darkness of the "dungeons."

As for the ghosts in the fort, Dori McMunn harbors only a hint of the skepticism she had regarding the supernatural before she took the position at the enchanted Fort Mifflin.

She cannot discount the reports from the guides, reenactors, visitors, and employees at the fort. She cannot deny that some very credible mediums and psychic researchers have come to some very convincing conclusions related to the cast of ghostly characters there.

"People claim to have taken pictures in the Casemates," Ms. McMunn said, "and somebody who wasn't there showed up in the pictures. I've seen some of those pictures, and it sure looks like it to me, but you never know."

"The Wissahickon is of so remarkable a loveliness that, were it flowing in England, it would be the theme of every bard...."

"Morning on the Wissahiccon"
Edgar Allan Poe

The Spirit of Summer Street

In the course of scouring the streets of the city for tips about places where spirits might dwell, the path to a ghost story can take unexpected turns.

Witness the random stop in the wonderfully-named "Ye Olde Original Bookfinders" used book store at 1018 Pine Street.

We posed the question to owner Bill Epler: "Know any ghost stories?" Simple, to the point.

His response was equally simple and to the point.

"No."

But as we browsed around his fine store in the heart of Antique Row, Epler, unbeknownst to us, had placed a phone call to a friend and neighbor up the street.

He handed us a slip of paper with a name and address on it, and suggested we pay a visit. "If anyone would know any ghost stories," Epler said, "he would."

The "he" was Joseph Sorger, who co-owns Sorger & Schwartz Antique Furniture & Decorative Arts at 1108 Pine—our next stop.

"Know any ghost stories?" Simple, to the point.

"Yes," he said.

Paydirt!

The affable Mr. Sorger readily took time from helping a steady flow of browsers and buyers and got right to *his* point—a terse but typical tale of what Sorger truly believes was an encounter with a ghost.

The retired architectural interior designer once owned a Greek Revival mansion at 1624 Summer Street. The building was designed by noted architect Thomas Ustick Walters (1804-1887), who also designed Founder's Hall at Girard College (1833), the Philadelphia Contributionship (1835), and the Senate and House wings of the U.S. Capitol in Washington (1833).

Joseph Sorger's experiences with the unknown began in 1963, shortly after he had purchased the sprawling property.

"On the second floor, in the evenings," he said, "there was a lady whose presence you could feel. It was benign—you never felt the least threatened. In fact, you felt quite comfortable.

"I used to think that I was the only one who felt her presence."

But that all changed when a house guest made a casual remark to Sorger.

"He had stayed in the house for about a year. He had a second floor bedroom, one of eight bedrooms in the house.

"He said to me one day, 'Did you ever notice anyone or feel anyone around this house?

"I asked him why he asked that question. He said it was because he was in the bathroom shaving, and he positively felt or heard something. When he looked around, there was no one there.

"He said he just knew that there was someone there. I asked if he knew if it was male or female. He said, oh, it was a lady. I asked if it was young or old. He said, well, maybe fifty or sixty years old."

Sorger said he only ever felt the presence, and never once saw it. "It was very strong," he noted.

"It didn't seem to be a servant or maid," he added. "It seemed like it was someone who was either the owner of the house or the wife of the owner."

Sorger remains philosophical about that encounter, and the eternal question about life after death.

He lost a good friend several years ago, but believes the spirit of the man still remains. "I still feel, even to this day," he said, "that there really is something to it all."

Sorger's former house was built around 1835, and he sold it to the Franklintown Corporation in 1976. That development firm demolished the stately structure to make way for a new building which stands there today.

And what *is* there today?

In the remote chance that you are reading this book in a room at the Wyndham Franklin Plaza Hotel, keep a close look over your shoulder–the old mansion, and its resident spirit, once occupied that very site.

Perhaps one of them still does!

ℒ

Ghosts of "The Great Road"

There is little dispute that as a singular geographical area within the city limits of Philadelphia, Germantown holds within it the most haunted places and the most ghost stories.

And, the "main street" of that sprawling and diverse neighborhood, Germantown Avenue, is lined with handsome historical mansions with many tales to tell.

Let us begin where, one might say, Germantown begins.

The Headless Woman of Cliveden

On six acres of parklike land at 6401 Germantown Avenue is Cliveden, the Georgian manor house built as a summer home by Benjamin Chew, the last British-appointed Chief Justice of Pennsylvania.

The exterior of its two-foot stone walls still hold scars from the Battle of Germantown which raged on around the property in September, 1777. And within those walls, folks have said for generations, are ghosts.

During the battle, 53 Colonial soldiers were killed in an attempt to capture the British-fortified mansion.

Do their spirits remain under the tall trees of Cliveden? Perhaps.

And then, there is the "headless woman" of Cliveden.

An old newspaper clipping, its date and source missing,

An old engraving of the Chew Mansion.

opened with the declaration:

"Everyone in Germantown knows that the Chew mansion is haunted."

We proceed from that rather profound pronouncement.

Tradition has it that an elderly woman who had been holed up inside the mansion during one of the skirmishes which preceded the major assault on Cliveden, became a grisly casualty.

According to the anonymous account, a crazed British soldier stationed in the mansion garrison, cut off the woman's head and ran from the house carrying it by its hair.

That headless woman, the story continued, could be seen by some, stumbling through the house and onto the lawns, searching for her severed head.

Justinia, the Ghost of Grumblethorpe

At 5267 Germantown Avenue is Grumblethorpe, which was built by merchant John Wister.

Its connection to the Battle of Germantown is strong, as British Gen. James Agnew chose it for his headquarters.

Gen. Agnew was mortally wounded during the battle, and was brought back to the Wister house, where he died.

Stains from his blood remain on the floor of the west parlor, near the "Courting Door."

It is believed that the general's ghostly energy remains at Grumblethorpe, as does the spirit of a less lofty personage.

A little girl named Justinia lost her parents during the yellow fever epidemic of 1793. The charitable Wisters took the orphan in and gave her a good home.

One of Justinia's passions was baking, and it is said that nearly every Friday night she would bake several loaves of bread which would be distributed to the poor the following morning.

Justinia's presence has been felt in the classic home ever since her death in about 1820. It is strongest after the sun goes down on a Friday night.

And, some say the sweet aroma of fresh bread can be detected wafting from Grumblethorpe from time to time.

Loudoun, ca. 1905.

Willie, Maria, and the
Many Ghosts of Loudoun

What would seem to be the most haunted house in the city of Philadelphia is Loudoun mansion, 4650 Germantown Avenue.

Built over a 30-year period beginning in 1801, Loudoun was named for Loudoun County, Va., ancestral home of the first owner, Thomas Armat.

The front porch of Loudoun rises on a promontory some 30 feet above an eastern plateau, which once afforded a commanding view of the city to the southeast. That view is now blocked by matured trees, and the mansion looks over a neighborhood which has seen better days.

Strong evidence supports the allegation that had Philadelphia been chosen as the capital of the United States, its capitol building would have been built where Loudoun is now.

Inside, many fine works of art, vintage wardrobes, furniture, and a brick-floored kitchen are Loudoun's strong points.

But for these pages, its very strongest points are its many ghosts.

Behold, if you will, "Little Willie."

Said to be William Armat Logan, son of a former owner, the reportedly retarded boy who, according to his mother's diary, "joined the angels" in 1860 at the age of eight. He was the son of Gustavus and Anna Logan, former owners of the home.

His restless spirit still roams the rooms of Loudoun, moving items and making things go bump in the night.

Little Willie's ghost has also been seen in the company of the spectral vision of a large, black dog.

In a handout prepared by the Loudoun Mansion in 1990, Willie was portrayed as "mischievous."

It was said that in life, Willie was often ordered to stand in the corner after he had been bad. Near one of the chimneys in the mansion, a cold spot has often been felt. It is believed it is the energy of "Little Willie."

He is also blamed for moving and hiding certain items, and later placing them where they don't belong. On several occasions, books on shelves and dinner sets in cabinets were shuffled, and "Little Willie" was deemed the culprit.

The second key player in the ghostly gallery at Loudoun is a man who married the daughter of Thomas Armat.

A mysterious shadow has been noticed on a staircase in the home, and it is believed to be the earthbound spirit of

James Skeritt (or Skerett).

Another ghost there is Maria Dickinson Logan, who was Willie's sister, and the last owner of the home (she died in 1939). Her apparition resides in what was her bedroom, and has been seen on several occasions by several witnesses.

Described in the Loudoun brochure as a "fierce spirit," Maria can be detected in her old bedroom. In that chamber, personal items which once belonged to Marie have often been found scattered, and a depression in the chaise lounge once signaled her sitting presence.

Maria, who maintained a stern disposition and was not known to be kind to her servants, still—in spirit form—has been known to make herself known to caretakers and maintenance workers at Loudoun.

The sun room of the spacious building is haunted by a woman in a rocking chair, and in the corridors of Loudoun, a pathetic spirit of a young waif wanders the night in an endless quest for a peaceful rest.

The sun room ghost has been described as a diminutive, older woman wearing a bonnet, and the little girl is believed to be about six or seven years old, dressed in early nineteenth century clothing, and prone to romping in the corridors of the big house.

The ghosts of Loudoun have attracted much attention over the years. Regional and national magazines have featured the phantoms in listings, and one declared it was one of fewer than three dozen houses in the United States with documented, "certified" hauntings.

A press release issued in the 1980s by the Pennsylvania Department of Commerce, Bureau of Travel Development, included "Little Willie" among the commonwealth's most important ghosts, and Loudoun has been featured in several books about America's most haunted places.

In Nancy Roberts' "Haunted Houses: Chilling Tales from Nineteen American Homes," stories of a "cloudy white light extending from the foot of a bed straight up to the ceiling" were told, as were accounts of filmy, glowing orbs which formed in certain rooms.

A woman who spent a night in Loudoun told the author she saw the vision of an older woman with a clenched fist sitting on the edge of a bed in Maria Logan's former bedroom.

In Dolores Riccio and Joan Bingham's "Haunted Houses USA," two more centers of energy were discussed.

A caretaker told the writers she had seen a "tall man dressed completely in black" materialize behind her. Startled, she asked him who he was, and before he could answer, the figure evaporated.

That incident could be related to what could be the most mysterious of all the ghosts at Loudoun–the untold Battle of Germantown casualties who suffered, died, and were interred on Neglee's Hill, upon which Loudoun was later built.

Maria Dickinson Logan willed the Federal-style mansion to the City of Philadelphia, which took over its administration in 1940. It was opened for limited touring in 1966, and several early visitors–many with no knowledge of any ghost stories there–claimed they were followed by unseen but strongly felt presences.

In a 1971 article in the Philadelphia *Evening Bulletin*, Mrs. John W. Farr, who was chair of the Friends of Loudoun, freely admitted that she and her committee members all believed there was a presence in the mansion.

"A number of things have happened for which there is no explanation," she was quoted as having said. "Some of the neighbors say that Miss Logan is guarding the property."

Of Ghost Ships and "Quarters A"

Friday, the 13th.

A thick oyster shell of a cloud wrapped a sinister shroud around the sun.

Surely it would pass quickly and golden beams of light and warmth would wrest the setting from the gloomy grip.

Rendered useless, my sunglasses were promptly removed and tucked into a jacket pocket.

In the same movement, I tightened the collar of the jacket as an icy chill penetrated fibers and flesh.

The cloud seemed stalled. The sun seemed forever cloaked.

I was at land's end in Philadelphia. And although cars and trucks rumbled on a bridge, trains clanked along nearby tracks, jets roared overhead, and tugs hooted in the distance, I was among ghosts. Many ghosts. Gray ghosts which floated silently before me, and a hulking white ghost which stood just over my shoulders.

111

• PHILADELPHIA GHOST STORIES •

I was between a ghost fleet of mothballed warships and a ghostly old building known only as "Quarters A."

I was just inside the main gate of the Philadelphia Naval Shipyard.

As the years play out beyond the publication of this book, wonderful things are expected to take place at the former Philadelphia Naval Shipyard at the southern tip of Broad Street where the Schuylkill and Delaware rivers meet.

In late 1997, public and private officials announced a huge deal which would bring thousands of jobs and a shipbuilding industry to the shipyard.

And, another partnership said it would establish a passenger cruise ship terminal at the yard.

Built in 1876 on what was then League Island, which was three miles–or one *league*–in circumference, the Navy shipyard closed in 1995 after more than a century of service to the military.

In its prime, the Philadelphia Navy Yard was the largest in the world and some 25,000 people worked there. It was a vital cog in America's defense system.

As an historic site, the "Navy Yard" left behind many memories for both civilians and sailors. And, it may have left behind a ghost or two.

Some call the Navy's reserve fleet in a Schuylkill River basin at the Navy Yard a "ghost fleet."

In that fleet at the time of the writing of this book were 55 ships in various stages of decline and disposition. They ranged from yard oilers to the battleship Iowa to the carriers Saratoga and Forrestal. To this writer, the one particularly haunting "ghost ship" in the fleet was the old destroyer, *USS Charles Adams.*

Some bound to become razor blades, some bound to be targets for gunnery practice, and some bound for maritime museums, the ships were lashed together, and stretched along forlorn piers.

Two ships which were not in this phantom flotilla were the U.S.S. Eldridge and U.S.S. The Sullivans. But their stories were the stuff legends are made of—each in its own way.

The Philadelphia ~~Experiment~~ Myth

For the sci-fi fans among you, be aware that it was at the Philadelphia Navy Yard, and aboard the U.S.S. Eldridge that the legendary "Philadelphia Experiment" allegedly took place.

The incident supposedly involved a top-secret Navy experiment in 1943 in which Einstein's "unified field" theory was employed and the Eldridge vanished from the Philadelphia pier and was teleported in a flash to Norfolk, Virginia. In another flash, the ship reappeared in Philadelphia.

Carlos Miguel Allende, of New Kensington, Pa., disclosed his "knowledge" of the experiment in 1955, and claimed he had witnessed the vanishing while on a ship in Norfolk harbor twelve years earlier.

Allende (a.k.a. Carl Allen) said he was aboard the merchant ship S.S. Andrew Furuseth when he saw the phenomenon take place.

Several books, movies, and Internet sites have perpetuated what the Office of Naval Research has called a "myth."

The most popular movie, a 1984 convoluted pyrotechnic thriller, featured not only the disappearance of the Eldridge, but its launch into cyberspace.

Filmed in Charleston, S.C., Salt Lake City, Utah, and Hollywood, "The Philadelphia Experiment" also featured Eldridge crewmen being melted into the steel decks of the ship, two sailors being time-warped 42 years into the future through an electromagnetic maelstrom which threatened the world, and witnesses watching the entire matter from aboard the U.S.S. Yorktown aircraft carrier.

There was no mention of the S.S. Furuseth or Carlos Allende, and no scenes filmed in Philadelphia.

The Navy checked the Eldridge's logs and found that the "tin can" was actually in New York harbor when the "witness" said he stood on the deck of the merchant ship and watched the navy vessel materialize in Norfolk.

What's more, the Navy further stated that the S.S. Andrew Furuseth wasn't in Norfolk harbor when Allende said he saw the teleportation.

Its promulgators said the experiment was code-named "Project Rainbow."

The ONR, in an official statement in 1996, said there *were* secret research experiments carried out in Philadelphia in 1943, but they involved "degaussing," which makes ships "invisible" to magnetic mines. Other "experiments" which could have created a sensation involved high-frequency generator tests which sometimes cast corona discharges.

The Navy flatly rejected any notion of any ship ever being "transported," and likened the wild stories to "whispering down the alley."

In its statement, the Office of Naval Research claimed it "never conducted any investigations on invisibility, either in 1943 or at any other time. There was a "Project Rainbow," but it was a war strategy, not an electronics experiment.

"In view of present scientific knowledge," the statement said, "ONR scientists do not believe that such an experiment could be possible except in the realm of science fiction."

It is interesting to note (and not necessarily *germane* to this story) that during World War II, three gentlemen who went on to successful careers as science fiction writers spent time working at the Navy Yard.

L. Sprague de Camp, Robert A. Heinlein, and Isaac Azimov each worked on the base at the time of the alleged "Philadelphia Experiment."

There is another story from the Navy Yard supernatural files which seems a bit more palatable.

The Ghost Ship

It was April, 1969, when a first class electrician's mate, Thomas Simmons, emerged from the U.S.S. The Sullivans with tales of bizarre occurrences he blamed on the ship's resident ghost

The ship was named to honor George, Francis, Madison, Albert, and Joseph Sullivan, brothers who enlisted together after a friend was killed aboard the U.S.S. Arizona at Pearl Harbor.

The Sullivan brothers asked to be assigned to the same ship, and in 1942 were all assigned to the U.S.S. Juneau.

Within the year, the Juneau was torpedoed by a Japanese sub and all five brothers were reported missing in action.

The Juneau was struck by the torpedo in November, 1942, but 140 crewmen survived the sinking. All but ten of those sailors, including the Sullivan brothers, died as the result of exposure or shark attacks in the waters off Guadalcanal Island.

The ship named for the brothers, 376-foot Fletcher-class destroyer, "The Sullivans" was launched in April, 1943, and was a battle-worn and decorated veteran of the Asiatic-Pacific campaigns in World War II and the Korean War before

The League Island Navy Yard, ca. 1910.

it was relegated to training status and then the mothball fleet along Davis Avenue in Philadelphia in 1965. Even in its retirement, the ship stood apart from the other gray ladies of the reserve basin because of the bright, green shamrocks which were painted on the forward smokestack.

The brothers' names are perpetuated in a second U.S.S. The Sullivans (DDG-68) which joined the fleet in April, 1997.

But it was aboard the old destroyer, and in Philadelphia, that EM1 Simmons said he was so shaken by an incident that he refused to ever board the The Sullivans ever again.

Simmons, who had been in the Navy twelve years, said he was standing on the bridge of the ship when a shipfitter's wrench glided in the air, past his head, and smacked into a nearby bulkhead.

He claimed there was no one else aboard the ship, and no one anywhere nearby, and was so baffled (read: scared) by the event that he scurried off the ship and shared his story with other sailors.

As it turned out, Simmons wasn't alone when it came to unexplainable incidents aboard the The Sullivans.

Voices echoing from within compartments and passageways, figures materializing and transporting through bulkheads, and at least one report of actual communication with a spirit on the ship—these things were quite common aboard the old ship, according to several civilian and military workers at the Navy Yard.

Those stories are hard to track down, but Gerry Miller, a South Philadelphia man whose father had worked at the Navy Yard, remembered his dad talking about it.

"All I remember," Miller said, "is that pop came home one day and mentioned to us kids that there was what he called a 'hoodoo ship' down in the yard.

"I remember the name, 'The Sullivans,' because pop told us about those unfortunate brothers. I also remember that he said he heard a lot of guys say they had weird things happen aboard the ship.

"He never had anything happen to him," Miller continued, "but he had a buddy who claimed to the day he died, on stacks of bibles, that he saw a sailor walking down the deck. He was wearing one of those old-fashioned hats sailors wore during the war, and the guy said the sailor sort of

117

turned around to look at him, and just disappeared into thin air!"

The "The Sullivans" was claimed by an historic ships organization and was moved from mothballs and into the Buffalo and Erie County Naval and Servicemen's Park in Buffalo, New York.

Apparently, the ship's ghosts decided to make the move, as well.

Scott Kodger, curator of the museum, said the ghosts "pop up every once in a while."

He said a maintenance worker at the museum was aboard the destroyer when he was tapped on the shoulder, looked around, and saw no one. Another employee who reported eerie sounds aboard the vessel flatly refuses to go aboard any more.

Kodger added that still another well-respected individual claimed he saw the figure of someone approach him on the ship—and watched in amazement and fear as that figure vanished into thin air!

Phantoms of the Forrestal

And while the destroyer has departed the "mothball fleet" of Philadelphia, another ship there at the time of this writing came stripped of its seaworthy *accouterments*, but equipped with ethereal beings which have been reported since at least the late 1980s.

It is the mighty aircraft carrier U.S.S. Forrestal, which at 1,086 feet is the largest of all ships in the Navy Yard.

The flattop reported to Philadelphia in 1993. Its ghosts were mustered in several years before then.

One of the phantoms of the Forrestal is a figure which appears and disappears on a fairly regular basis. It's believed it is the ghost of a former chief petty officer who was killed in a 1967 fire which claimed 137 lives aboard the ship.

Stories of ghosts on the Forrestal have been reported from sources as reliable as the Associated Press and as questionable as supernatural sites on the internet.

The AP article of 1988 related the experiences of various sailors as detailed in a 12-page news release issued by a Forrestal lieutenant.

In the document, eyewitnesses claimed that storage areas well below the hangar deck are the lairs of the ghost.

Doors opened and closed with no human aid, and a second-class petty officer said he saw a ghost dressed in khaki descend a ladder into a pump room—and never come back out.

Another incident involved a faint, mysterious voice which was heard over a telephone on the bridge.

The phone rang, and a sailor answered. "Help! Help! I'm on the sixth deck!," a quivering voice exclaimed over the phone....which, the sailor soon discovered, was disconnected!

Several Forrestal crewmen reportedly chose to disobey orders rather than enter certain areas of the ship which were deemed as haunted.

Do ghosts still roam the decks of the Forrestal? Anyone willing to find out?

Quarters A

There are many fine buildings in the sprawling old Navy Yard, but none as fine as the one just inside the main gate—the gleaming, white "Quarters A."

One of the first buildings to be erected on League Island during construction of the Navy Yard (1874-75), Quarters A was the residence of the officer in charge of the project.

It was later used as VIP quarters for visiting dignitaries and was lavishly furnished with period furniture during that elegant time of its existence.

In the late 1980s, the building was used as a temporary Officers' Club while the base club was undergoing renovations. After a short period in that capacity, Quarters A was abandoned.

It is one of Philadelphia's least-known and least-seen historic buildings.

Added to the National Register of Historic Places in 1976 and recorded in the Historic American Buildings Survey, Quarters A has been hailed by architectural experts for its detailed Italianate Villa features and for its simple elegance.

Readers of this book may well imagine ghosts streaming from its corner tower, or shadows passing by the windows of its semi-octagonal bay window.

Quarters A *looks* haunted.

And, in stories passed down over the decades down in the Navy Yard, it very well may *be* haunted.

The story has been passed on for several years, but no baseline could be established.

What could be determined is that the spirits which wander in and around Quarters A are those of two seamen, whose sometimes shadowy, sometimes glowing figures have been seen on the grounds, sometimes accompanied by the form of a ghostly, black dog.

"Quarters A" is said to be haunted by the spirits of two sailors.

121

Sautter's Main Gate Luncheonette is haunted by "Uncle George," according to its owner and employees.

The Ghost of the Main Gate Luncheonette

Not all Philadelphia landmarks date to the days Thomas Jefferson strolled the streets. Benjamin Franklin isn't associated with every historic site in town.

This, after all, is a city which considers several of its cheesesteak joints as historical sites. A city where there's an official marker where the "American Bandstand" TV show originated–a city where serious historians can document street corners where Bobby Rydell and Fabian hung out–a city with a Mummers' Museum.

Such is the stuff of a city deep with history and steeped in pride.

• PHILADELPHIA GHOST STORIES •

There are bona fide landmarks within the walls and fences of the old Navy Yard at the foot of Broad Street. And, there's one just outside its main gate.

It is, appropriately, the Main Gate Luncheonette, and most sailors and civilians who have spent any amount of time at the Navy Yard since the 1920s has either passed by or stopped into the luncheonette at one time or another.

Utilitarian in design, what is actually *Sautter's* Main Gate Luncheonette is situated on the east side of Broad Street—or, at least at the time of this writing was. With numerous plans for development of the former Navy Yard on the boards at that time, the fate of Sautter's hung in the balance.

But at that time, early 1998, Denise and Bob Sautter were busy as the seventh-generation Sautters tending the popular breakfast and lunch place.

Your author stopped in to ask if anyone at the luncheonette knew anything at all about the stories at "Quarters A," which is visible across Broad Street from Sautter's.

Denise Sautter said she had heard the stories, and told us what she knew.

But then, she threw a curve.

"Yeah," she said, "we have a ghost in this place, too."

She wasn't kidding.

Denise had seen a lot in her 13 years at the Main Gate. And, she'd become quite familiar with a phantom she and others there called "Uncle George."

The name was more than a sobriquet for the spook.

"Uncle George" was Francis ("Everybody called him 'Uncle George'") Sautter, who operated the luncheonette

123

just before Denise and Bob took it over.

Sometimes quite demonstrative but never threatening, Uncle George's spirit makes itself known in many ways.

In fact, Denise said that just before our visit to the luncheonette, a few pots and pans had flown off shelves.

"Uncle George," Denise said as she shook her head in affirmation.

"It's a lot of little things," she added. "Noises, odd things that happen. Like the shower in the back of the restaurant—sometimes it has turned itself on or off. Things like that."

Sharon Grosso, an employee at Sautter's, said she, too, has come across Uncle George.

On one occasion, she was in the luncheonette alone for a little more than an hour, waiting for her boyfriend to pick her up.

"We had a dish washer who used to stay late once in a while," she remembered. "And although I knew I was there all alone, I heard the sound of somebody scraping pots and pans up front. I said, 'Barb!' [the dish washer's name]

"Then, I walked out into the kitchen and the lights all went out and there was not a soul in there."

Except, she quipped, Uncle George.

"Yeah," she continued, "I got a really eerie feeling."

Grosso said she knows Uncle George is a benevolent ghost, but antics she attributed to him often catch her off guard.

"One time," she said, "I was sitting in the back room and I felt somebody actually pull me almost out of the chair. I really think it was Uncle George."

Sharon, Denise, and anyone else who has crossed paths

with the playful ghost can be confused, but are generally comfortable with it.

"I knew Uncle George," Denise said. "And he was a good, good, good man," Denise said. "He practically lived here."

And perhaps, in a sense, he still does.

"Rate a Wraith?"

Many hours of research for this book were spent in the back racks of historical societies, the deep bins of libraries, and on the streets of the city.

But sometimes, leads to ghost stories come from the most unexpected places.

Take, for example, the pages of a newspaper not usually on file in respected libraries. Take, for example, the *National Enquirer*.

Ghost stories are a dime a dozen in the tabloids, but one, cut out and saved by a Philadelphia man who shared it with the author, was special.

In July 1956, a 26-year old upstate New Yorker and WFIL radio (560-AM) afternoon disc jockey named Dick Clark took over for Bob Horn as host of a local television show called "Bandstand." Horn, who was discharged from the show for reasons which remain controversial, had founded the show in 1952.

On August 5, 1957, 48 ABC network stations bought into Clark's concept that the teenage dance and music show could catch on across the country. It did, and Philadelphia soon became the epicenter for all which was "cool," "hip," or "hep" to teenagers.

Seven years after that, however, "American Bandstand"

left the old WFIL-TV (channel six) studios at 46th and Market Sts. and headed west to a sound stage and dance floor in Los Angeles.

Clark left in his wake many broken-hearted Philly teens, and a legacy which proved to be so strong that a Pennsylvania historical marker has been placed at the old WFIL building, which when built in 1947, was among the very first structures in the United States built solely for television production.

He also left behind a minor but, considering the source, tidy little ghost story.

The *Enquirer* broke the short story in 1985 as "Dick Clark's Incredible Psychic Experience."

The gist of the story is that Clark, while walking down a hallway in the WFIL studios at around 11 o'clock in the morning, met a co-worker who had been very ill. He asked the man how he was feeling, and the man said he was getting better, but still not up to par.

A couple of nights later, Clark bumped into the man's son at a social gathering. He told him that he had seen his father and that he had seemed to be doing and looking just fine.

When the son asked Clark to repeat the time he said he saw the man, Clark said it was 11 a.m.

The son was shocked. He proceeded to tell Clark that at 11 a.m. that day, his father was on a table in an operating room of a city hospital, and his heart stopped. His father, he assured Clark, could not have been at WFIL. But Clark was certain it was that man he saw in that hallway on that morning.

In his "Ghosts of the Rich and Famous," author Arthur Myers tracked down a Raleigh, N.C., radio talk show host who had spoken to Dick Clark about the incident.

With slight variations, Clark had confirmed the experience as reported earlier in the *Enquirer*.

An historical marker stands at the former WFIL studios in West Philadelphia.

The Ghost Hunters' Ghost Stories

Much of the groundwork for this book was laid by the founders of the Philadelphia Ghost Hunters Alliance, Lewis and Sharon Gerew.

And what led them to establish such an organization for the investigation and documentation of supernatural events in and around Philadelphia?

What prompted it were some inexplicable experiences the Gerews had in both their single lives, and their lives as a married couple.

The stories are best told in their own words:

"While living in the historic Tacony section of northeast Philadelphia," Lew Gerew said, "ghosts have made their presence known to my wife and me for many years.

"In fact, I would consider the number of times we have actually experienced ghostly activity to be abnormally high.

"One entity in particular made several appearances and left us with a lasting impression."

Sharon Gerew has been able to sense spirit activity since a very early age.

"Call me crazy," she mused, "but I believe I attract them somehow."

She spoke of that "one entity in particular" which entered their lives before they were married and was a prime

129

motivator of the Gerews' efforts to organize the PGHA.

"I was just coming from the store," she related, "and heading back to my house, which was right around the corner from Lew's parents' home. As I headed toward their place I was somehow drawn to look up to the second floor window, which at the time was Lew's bedroom.

"As I looked up, I saw my mother-in-law standing in the window with the curtain pulled aside so she could wave out to me.

"I waved back to her. Once we exchanged waves she moved back from the window and fixed the curtain to its proper position. I then thought of the countless times she had scolded me for not stopping by to say hello. She always said, 'Ya know, Lew doesn't have to be the only reason that you stop by!'

"So, I decided to pay her a visit before I went home. I must have knocked for at least a minute when I finally decided to go home. For some reason, she wasn't answering the door. Maybe, I thought, she had still been upstairs and didn't hear me knocking. So, I left.

"Five o'clock rolled around and I decided to head on over to see Lew. As soon as I got there I asked his mother why she didn't answer the door after she had seen me earlier.

"She looked at me rather strangely and asked at what time that took place. I told her it was around 12:30 p.m. Once again, she looked at me as if she had no idea what I was talking about and replied that she had been at her crafts lesson from about 11 a.m. to 3 p.m.

"We were both puzzled. I knew that I had seen her. Or had I?

"I didn't even consider anything about a ghost until

much later on, when both Lew and I saw that same woman again on at least three occasions."

Lew has also seen the woman's ghost. Both he and Sharon agree that the spirit could easily pass as his mother. But, there may be another baseline for the alleged haunting.

"The woman who lived in that house before my in-laws," Sharon added, "choked to death and died in the house. Could it be her? We find it very strange that the ghost looks so much like Lew's mother, though. And *she* is very much alive!"

Lew continued with another encounter which took place in his parents' old house in Tacony.

"It was about 4:30 in the morning, and my turn to warm up some formula for our three-week old son. I jumped out of bed and went downstairs.

"It was quite strange for me to be as alert as I was that early. As I reached the bottom of the steps, I turned toward the dining room. As I turned, I saw a figure in the dining room, peering out the window.

"The window shade was only half drawn, leaving a sizable space to look out from.

"I stopped in my tracks. For a brief moment, I thought it was my mother. The streetlight glow was entering the window, so there was no doubt that someone was there.

"Then, I saw a glimmer of movement, as if weight was being shifted from one foot to the other.

"Frozen in place, I called to her. The first call was a little soft, as to not wake anyone else in the house. With no response, I tried louder the second time, realizing that my mother had been having a hearing problem.

"Without a word, the figure stood erect, seeming to

acknowledge that it knew that I was there. More frightening was the fact that although the light was still coming into the window, the figure took on a menacing black appearance. The color was such a deep black that it almost seemed like a void in the silhouette of a person.

"At that point I was getting alarmed. The only comfort I found was the fact that we were separated by a rather large dining room table and about 25 feet of distance.

"Suddenly, it moved closer. My adrenaline surged. I was convinced we had an intruder. I prepared for battle. Slowly, and never straying from facing my opponent, I walked to a light switch a few feet away.

"In anticipation of what faced me, I clicked on the switch.

"There was no one there. It disappeared as the light went on.

"I took a deep breath, made my son his bottle, told Sharon what happened, and....went to bed."

Just another night in the life of a ghost hunter!

A Voice in Betsy's Basement

She should more properly be known as Elizabeth Claypoole, and more than likely her most important contribution to history is that she designed flags for the Pennsylvania Navy.

But in historical myth, that gray area between fact and fiction, she is Betsy Ross, and she is credited with the sewing of the first stars and stripes.

It is a comfortable image—little Betsy, crouched over a broad swath of cloth, laboriously stitching the red, white, and blue that would fly as a symbol of freedom far beyond the expectations of those in her world, in her time.

The Betsy Ross myths notwithstanding, the old (circa 1740) home known popularly as the Betsy Ross House (actually the American Flag House/Betsy Ross Memorial) is a popular and worthwhile stop along Philadelphia's history trail.

Ross probably never lived there, and probably never worked there. Perhaps her work wasn't nearly as important as its legend purports. But that's all right—America needs good, strong legends like Betsy.

One thing is for certain, while Ross, or Claypoole, or Griscom, or Ashburn, may never have lived there, she *is* buried there.

And maybe, just maybe, her spirit remains there eternally.

The "Betsy Ross House," ca. 1905.

• PHILADELPHIA GHOST STORIES •

It is known that Elizabeth Griscom was born New Year's Day, 1752 to Quaker parents. It is known that she became a seamstress and upholsterer and was hired by the Pennsylvania legislature, Benjamin Franklin, and the Society of Free Quakers. And it is quite conceivable that she might have had a hand in the designing and/or sewing of the first flag of the United States.

The truth, alas, is long lost in historical distortion.

Betsy Griscom-Ashburn-Ross-Claypoole is buried with her last husband, John Claypoole, in a courtyard of the house. Her first two husbands were casualties of the Revolutionary War.

It was Charles H. Weisgerber who, in 1893, founded the American Flag House and Betsy Ross Memorial Association.

An accomplished artist and historian, Weisgerber lived in the old house at 239 Arch Street for nearly 30 years and died there in 1932.

Arthur M. Holst, executive director of the house and memorial at the time of this writing, takes immense pride in the legend of Betsy Ross, the lure of the house and memorial (some 300,000 visitors streamed through in the year prior to publication of this book), and works hard to maintain the image of the historic property.

And he is hard-pressed to explain some of the odd incidents which have taken place there since he became director in 1996.

The director said he has heard stories about hauntings in the house.

"A psychic visited here one time," he recalled, "and claimed that Betsy Ross herself still resides in the house. They say her ghost has been seen, or sensed, sitting at the foot of her bed. And, they say, for some reason she is upset."

Several employees have heard what they can best describe as "voices" in the basement of the house, and both Holst and assistant manager Gregory D. Bell admit that there are many times they look over their shoulders as if someone is watching them.

"One time," Holst said, "I was in the basement, and I distinctly heard someone say 'pardon me.' There was no one there, and there was no doubt in my mind what I heard.

"I told one of the gift shop workers about it," he continued. "I remember that I heard it, looked around, and was almost relieved that there was nobody there. It was, shall I say, memorable."

Holst speculated that the voice may well have been that of the benevolent spirit of Mr. Weisgerber, who so loved the old house and may have chosen to stay around awhile.

The kitchen in the basement of the Betsy Ross House.

Ghosts of the INN

It is one of Philadelphia's wonderful, hidden restaurants in one of Philadelphia's wonderful, hidden neighborhoods.

Call it "Washington Square West," call the "Arts District," call it what you may, but the tangle of tight streets and walkways between Walnut, Spruce, 12th and 13th Street is pure Philadelphia, and purely intriguing.

Coursing the midsection of the neighborhood is Camac Street–the last wooden block street in the United States (the blocks are still under the blacktop).

One would never know it by looking at Camac Street today, but its single traffic lane has a checkered past.

A tunnel beneath the street was likely a shelter for the transit of slaves through the "Underground Railroad" during the Civil War.

For a while, Camac Street was the center of a district of bawdy houses and bordellos which collectively made up the city's notorious "Latin Quarter."

A successful cleanup campaign restored order to the neighborhood, and through the last century Camac and surrounding streets have become center-city showcases.

The Sketch Club and the Plastic Club, two of the oldest art clubs in America, are located on Camac, as is the renowned women's theatrical club, the Charlotte Cushman Club.

Several ghosts roam the INN Philadelphia restaurant on Camac St.

And, a pair of Federal-style townhouses at Camac and Manning Streets have, since the beginning of the 20th century, housed a succession of highly-regarded restaurants.

The Poor Richard's Club was housed there, as was one of the city's first French restaurants, the private Le Coin d'Or.

In the mid-1970s, the buildings became the Camp Williamsburg Inn, another private club; and from 1978 to 1987, they encompassed Deux Cheminees, a fine French restaurant.

After a fire extensively damaged that restaurant in 1987, the buildings were vacant until 1993, when George Lutz and Phil Orchowski purchased them and began a thorough restoration which resulted in the partners' superb restaurant and bar, INN Philadelphia.

Hailed by food critics (including a Lambda Award as the Best Restaurant in Philadelphia) and highly-regarded for its decor, the INN Philadelphia comprises a comfortable lobby with two of the buildings' five fireplaces, a cozy piano bar, the elegant Franklin and Green dining rooms, and a brick wall-lined, lavishly-landscaped "Secret Garden" dining area out back.

And, as you may have guessed, INN Philadelphia has a ghost...or two....or more.

The lineage of the neighborhood, the street, and the ca. 1824-25 restaurant buildings is important to their character, and to the characters who, both George and Phil believe, haunt them.

Both rational and sensible men, with backgrounds in construction and microbiology, the owners of the INN are firmly convinced there are playful, demonstrative, and perhaps melancholy spirits there.

*Chandeliers in the "Franklin Room" have been known to move on their
own, and spirits have been detected in the lovely
dining room of INN Philadelphia.*

"We've had significant incidents here," Lutz said.

It was about three weeks before the INN was to open, in the summer of 1994 when the native Philadelphian was alone in a basement office.

"I heard a very heavy footfall right over my head," he continued.

Lutz described the sound as a *step/drag...step/drag*. He had no thoughts whatsoever about ghosts at the time. He feared there was an intruder upstairs.

"I got brave with my tear gas canister and started to nose around a bit. I began slowly and cautiously going through the building. I found absolutely nothing out of order."

The restaurateur was relieved, but puzzled. But, a few months after the INN opened, there may have been a revelation.

"A previous owner of the property came in for dinner with his lady friend," he continued. "At her urging, he mentioned that when he was preparing to open his restaurant (Deux Cheminees) here 15 years before my ownership, his father, who had helped in the rebuilding of the property, had passed away shortly before the opening.

"He said his father, who was a carpenter, loved the building, and had sort of a kinship with the property."

In their tableside conversation, the prior owner spoke fondly of his deceased dad, and mentioned in passing that he always wore very heavy boots and walked with a very pronounced limp.

Step/drag....step/drag....step/drag?

In another incident, a bartender and manager were closing up at the end of the night when the bartender, in a second-floor changing room, heard the adjacent women's room door open and close. He then heard the doors to the two main dining rooms open and close.

Spooked, he went downstairs and summoned the manager. The two carefully went back upstairs to investigate, only to discover a sight which froze them dead in their tracks.

As the manager slowly opened the door to the Franklin Room, both mens' eyes were drawn to the heavy, brass chandeliers, which were swinging gently but quite noticeably in opposite directions.

"The bartender said 'What the (blank)) is going on?' And with that, the chandeliers stopped swinging back and forth and started rotating in circles!"

The manager beat a hasty retreat back downstairs and found the stereo sound system was turned on at peak level. He was certain he had, just moments before, turned the system off.

"They just set the alarms," Lutz said, "and left the building."

Several employees have had encounters with whatever energies may swirl at INN Philadelphia.

"It wasn't until six or seven months after our opening," Lutz continued, "that I learned that our prep people who come in early in the day wouldn't leave the parameters of the downstairs kitchen, only because they said they were very annoyed and somewhat afraid of footsteps and voices they say they'd heard on the second floor."

As Lutz, Orchowski, and the staff grew more comfortable with the buildings and their unseen inhabitants, those spirits made themselves known to others.

"We've had incidents when customers have reported things," Lutz said.

"One time, two folks, both in the financial investment business, both very rational people, were here. The woman claimed she had her hair pulled twice while seated at the table. The first time she thought it was a server, but her husband, who had been looking at her at the time, said there was nobody there.

"She mentioned the incident to her server, who told me about it. So, I went over to their table and explained to them that sometimes we have strange but non-threatening occurrences."

Phantom footfalls, disembodied voices, even swinging chandeliers—stock, standard stuff for haunted places. But there's more—much more—to come.

Not long before this book was published (Lutz said that profound supernatural incidents take place there about every five or six weeks), Lutz had been seated at the bar with eight or nine customers in for the Sunday brunch.

"As I was talking to a friend, facing away from the other people, my friend's face took on an ashen look. His jaw dropped, and he said 'What the (blank) was that??

"As I turned, whatever he and the other people were seeing, was gone!

"Evidently, a form had come out of our coat room, walked between the bar and piano, and faded into the Camac Street wall of our building!

"It was quite amazing. I looked at those people, and they were absolutely stupefied!"

George Lutz said that none of those in attendance for that very perplexing episode knew anything about any prior

143

ghostly incidents at the INN.

But those incidents continued, on several levels of the building and of psychic activity.

A picture which hung on one wall of a second floor corridor flipped from that wall and struck the opposite wall, several feet away. Dishes "flew" from racks in the kitchen. Footfalls and voices became commonplace.

But the most telling moments in the supernatural saga of the superb restaurant came when a pair of patrons with heightened "awareness" came to call.

"They told me they had 'seen' many people, including children, in the building," Lutz said, as his demeanor took on a more serious tone.

The spirit energy seemed strongest in a stairway which leads to the "Secret Garden" and in the second floor dining rooms.

"From what I was told, there are ghosts of three adults and two children in the building. They are mostly concentrated on the second floor, but on the fourth floor of our south building there is a tremendous sense of sadness.

"Now, the person who detected that 'sadness' could not have known this, but I had earlier discovered that there may have been a rather serious fire on that upper level—well before the 1987 fire here—because there were remnants of charred roof beams which had been covered over."

Lutz's own psychic awareness has become raised significantly through his years at the INN. At one point, he contacted serious paranormal researchers and suggested a séance be conducted there.

"Both of the psychics advised against that. They said it could lend strength for the spirits to materialize and possibly cause more serious problems. We'd never had any overt signs of hostility, and I certainly didn't want any.

"So, I asked my manager, my chef, and my partner, and we took a vote on the séance. They quickly and unanimously said 'no'....let's just not go there!"

Respecting their wishes, George Lutz resolved that he would deal with whatever the ghosts sent his way.

He recalled one incident when, after a live jazz band had played for a wedding reception there, the level of "activity" seemed to increase. Perhaps, he thought, the spirits were mounting a protest against the type, or the volume of the music.

Lutz had had enough. He, after all, was the boss there, and would have none of any ghosts interfering with or demonstrating against the normal course of business.

"Once," he said, "I went into the Franklin dining room. In a very strong voice I said, 'Whoever you are, you are welcome to stay here. My home is your home.

"'As long as you do no damage and never hurt anybody, you are welcome to stay as long as you choose.'"

"I gave the ghosts a caveat, though," he continued. "I told it, "If you do harm the property or people, then what I am going to do is play the music as loud as I can...I'm going to turn the temperature up as high as it can get, or as low as I can get it...

"'...and I'm going to do the best I can to make whatever lives you have very, very miserable!

"So let's be friends!"

Mediums who have visited INN Philadelphia say George's firm warnings may have been effective.

One person with psychic abilities confirmed several very

strong energies in the buildings, including but not limited to the three adults, two children, and the *step/drag* man.

None of the spirits, however cranky and cantankerous they may seem at times, can or would do any harm.

"They'd (blank) well better not," warned George Lutz.

Cresheim Cottage Cafe, 7402 Germantown Avenue, around the turn of the 20th century.

Emily, the Ghost of Cresheim Cottage

They call her Emily.

"They" are those who work in, and have worked on a pleasant little restaurant known as the Cresheim Cottage Cafe.

Another of Philadelphia's truly remarkable and "hidden" treasures, Cresheim Cottage dates to around 1748, and, as is stated on its menu, "witnessed the first shots of the Battle of Germantown on October 4, 1777, when the American Colonial troops fired on British pickets...and these same Colonial troops made a hasty retreat along the 'Great Road.'"

That "Great Road," is now Germantown Avenue, and it is along that historic thoroughfare, where Mt. Airy and Chestnut Hill meet, that the cafe has watched history pass in review.

"Yeomen, lawyers, butchers, weavers, stocking knitters,

hatters, furriers, powder makers, printers, victualers, a sheriff, a judge and nurserymen have all made Cresheim Cottage their home," the menu story continues.

Also making the cottage its home these days is little Emily, its resident ghost.

The story is best told by Kathy Detwiler, a server at the cafe:

"One day, one of the nieces of the previous owner came into the restaurant and asked if we had seen any ghostly activity here.

"So of course, we asked what she meant, and she said that upstairs, she was walking past one of the bathrooms and she saw a girl in the corner.

"Well, of course, she stopped and looked, and there—standing in a corner as if she had been bad—was a young girl, maybe ten or eleven years old.

"She had long, dark hair done in Victorian style, and was wearing a pink Victorian dress.

"While the lady watched, the child disappeared before her eyes!"

As the story spread through the ranks at Cresheim Cottage Cafe, the workers there linked that sighting with many unexplainable incidents which had taken place there.

"We called our ghost 'Emily,'" Ms. Detwiler added.

Ken Weinstein, the owner of the care, acknowledges and accepts Emily's presence.

"We use Emily as a way of explaining things that happen," he said. "We think of her as a mischievous little girl, but very friendly and not dangerous or anything."

Thus, whenever a light turns itself on or off, whenever an appliance is fidgety, whenever something disappears and reappears mysteriously—it's the work of Emily.

Weinstein was personally introduced to the presence in the cafe by a woman who lived up the street and had done a historical review of the cottage for the local parish newsletter.

The writer gave Weinstein a copy of the newsletter, and noted that there was a section—a section about the ghostly sighting by the previous owner, a Mrs. Ernst—which had been, for whatever reason, edited out of the story.

Emily has always been sighted or sensed on the second floor, which is a later (probably around the turn of the 19th century) addition to the original structure.

It is interesting to note that in addition to the original sighting by the previous owner, and the random and sundry incidents where present staff members have met "Emily," another raft of sightings came from a most unexpected source.

"When we were remodeling here in 1996," Weinstein pointed out, "the contractors, on at least three occasions, spotted what they called a 'short shadow.' They said it was a ghost.

"They didn't know it was a girl, necessarily, until it came out later that Mrs. Ernst had also seen the spirit."

Weinstein believes "Emily" emerged from her eternal plane because of the sweeping alterations which were being made to the interior.

"That's my guess," Weinstein said, "because we disrupted this old house for her."

That keen observation by the cafe owner speaks to the very question of the existence of ghosts.

Let us use "Emily" as a springboard for a deeper

discussion on that subject.

Who of us could ever offer proof positive that somehow, somewhere, on some other plane or in some parallel time, we share our world with spirits...specters...with phantoms...with *ghosts?*

Then again, who can prove we do not?

Do ghosts exist? Do you—*do I*—believe in ghosts?

Do clouds exist? We can see clouds, but we cannot touch them. We cannot capture them in jars and bring them back to earth as proof they are real.

Does the wind exist? Wind we cannot see, but we can feel it as a gentle breeze or a terrifying blast.

Do I, as one who has chronicled the carryings-on of these ghoulies and ghosties for 30 years, *believe* in those ghoulies and ghosties?

Does it matter?

One must face the reality of death, and therefore I believe one must face the proposition that while the human *animal* must perish, the human *animus* may indeed remain.

What was flesh and bone may become dust. But, what were electrical charges in the nervous system may continue as information-laden impulses which stay, suspended and circulating in an eternal swirl of a magnetic field.

Could these impulses—these shards of emotions and information from a dead body—then *record* themselves somehow on something?

As in simple tape recording, could not these invisible pulses possibly become attracted to and deposited on ferrous oxide—*rust?*

Could these scientifically-rational and conceivable electrical charges which burst from their corporeal confines at the time of extreme trauma be the seeds of the supernatural? Could these bits and pieces be *ghosts?*

If there is one thicker thread which weaves its way through nearly every tale I have investigated in Philadelphia and throughout the world, it is that on virtually every "case" the building in which the haunting took or is taking place has been renovated or altered in some way, as in the case of the Cresheim Cottage Cafe.

Could any kind of severe trauma—such as, but not limited to, death—which may have taken place in those places have resulted in the bursting from the body of those impulses, and the recording of those impulses on rust?

Could the renovation have disturbed that recording by exposing the rust and allowing an unwary psychic mind to push the "playback" button and detect these impulses?

As inconceivable as this may be to some, so is the proposition that living faces and forms and voices and sounds could be recorded on strips of plastic and retrieved on a glass screen or paper speaker.

But those are the wonders we call audio and video, which in an electronic age seem all so natural.

The anonymous author of a 1867 book, *Ghost Stories: Collected With A Particular View To Counteract The Vulgar Belief In Ghosts And Apparitions,* which attempted to dispel the notion of ghosts, did pose an interesting question.

But what does a ghost represent? What is it the ghost of? Of a man or woman, to be sure. But does it appear as a man or woman only? Is it nude? Oh no! Shocking! This is contrary to all the rules. It always appears dressed.

If the man has been murdered, it appears in the very clothes he was murdered in, all bloody, with pale, murdered-looking face, and a ghastly wound in the breast, head, stomach, back or abdominal region.

If the person died quietly a natural death, in bed; then the ghost is generally clad in long white robes, or a shroud.

So then, we have the ghost of the clothes also-the ghost of the coat and unmentionables-the ghost of the cocked hat and wig?   How is this?

A viable query. If, as is almost always the case, a ghost does "return" to earth fully clothed, does that mean that cotton...wool...a belt or hat, shoes or socks...or polyester...rise from the grave and "return" as well?

Not likely. But, as human beings with certain levels of intellect, imagination, and anticipation, we tend to animate, illustrate, and clothe our psychic visitors.

What "returns" is merely a psychic signal which, in accordance with historical or emotional tradition, is given its toggery and its temperament by the more practical side of the psychic mind.

Thus, "Emily" (or whatever the unfortunate waif's real name may have been) appears as a ghost in a pink Victorian dress to some, but a "short shadow" to others.

Does a Victorian girl's spirit haunt Cresheim Cottage? Many people say yes.

That notion has permeated the mindsets of several folks who work there. And although "Emily" is a harmless and almost romantic lass, her presence has made a profound impact.

Kathy Detwiler said she is a bit uneasy when she goes upstairs in the cottage, and tries to never be up there alone.

Is "Emily" the only spirit of Cresheim Cottage? Perhaps not.

• PHILADELPHIA GHOST STORIES •

As Ms. Detwiler recalled, "One time a psychic came in and she sat in our fireplace room.

"She told us there was a very strong presence there. It was a woman. And, she said....it doesn't like men!"

So, is the Cresheim Cottage Cafe—or, for that matter, anyplace in Philadelphia—haunted?

Can anyone who believes it is actually prove it *is?*

Can anyone who believes it is not actually prove it *is not?*

Therein lies the mystery, the *wonder* of it all.

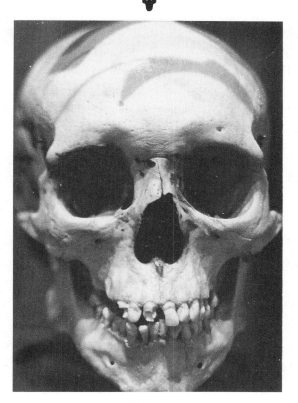

Is this one of the ghosts of Baleroy, photographed by the author?

Baleroy:
The Most Haunted House In Philadelphia

I shall state it simply. Throughout nearly 30 years of investigating haunted places across the world, I have never ventured into a home as spell-binding as Baleroy, and have rarely met anyone as fascinating as the man who calls the 30-room mansion home.

Called one of the most haunted places in America, the Chestnut Hill home of George Gordon Meade Easby is, without any doubt, the most haunted place in Philadelphia.

It was on what the Irish call a "soft day" when our investigative team was granted a rare tour of the property and an unforgettable audience with its personable "squire."

Meade Easby is a direct descendent of Gen. George Meade, who was the Battle of Gettysburg hero and the designer of Barnegat, Cape May, and several other lighthouses. The broad branches of his family tree also extend into the Mifflin, Rockefeller and Stevenson families, and his interests are as diverse and deep as has been his life experiences.

With vigor and vitality belying his 79 years, Easby ushered us through the lived-in museum which has been his home since childhood.

Easby's plush white hair tousled over an ever-smiling face and bid us welcome in the reception room.

It wasn't long until we were introduced to one of the ghosts—the many ghosts—of Baleroy.

As we exchanged cordialities, I passed a stunning Robert Shearman tall case clock. Its door was opened. Odd, I thought, in an otherwise tidy and orderly entrance hall.

That door, I learned later, is a plaything of one of the ghosts.

But soon, even more ominous events were to unfold.

As Easby ushered us to a beautiful room to the right of the entrance hall, his voice was firm: "Welcome," he stated, "to the most haunted room in the house!"

The most haunted room in the most haunted house in Philadelphia—and quite possibly the United States! We settled in for what would be an unforgettable experience.

It was in that Blue Room, furnished in the style of an 18th century drawing room, where we were to discuss the ghosts of Baleroy over wine and hors d'oeuvres.

It was in the elegant chamber where Easby urged us to sit, to be comfortable, to relax.

"But I'd advise you to not sit in that chair," Easby noted, gesturing to a blue winged-back chair.

"That," he said blithely, "is the death chair. It's the only chair I advise guests never to sit in."

A silken rope is draped over the chair, marking it off-limits. Not because it is particularly rare (in a home furnished by items once owned by the likes of Napoleon, Jefferson, and various world monarchs), but because the last three individuals who sat in the chair died within days of doing so.

Coincidence? Curse? Why test it?

After settling into comfortable seats, our eyes darted about (to the oil lamp from Pompeii, the Chippendale sofa mirror, the Charles Willson Peale portraits, etc., etc., etc.) as Meade Easby introduced us to his myriad "house guests."

Actually, we were introduced to them in a pair of handouts Easby provided us upon arrival.

One sheet, entitled "Baleroy: Adventure Into the Unknown," listed nearly two dozen mysterious events and artifacts in the mansion/museum...

• *Many people have seen ectoplasm in the house in the form of a faint white fog*

• *There is often a "barrier," or negative pressure that can be felt on entering certain rooms*

• *A guest was hit on the head with a bowl from a mantel piece*

....things like that.

And, oh yes, one that peaked my interest right quickly...

• *A tall case clock in the hall unlocked and the door opened wide*

Sure enough, as we spoke, all of us gathered in the Blue Room, that clock door somehow closed and latched itself—a phenomenon we all noticed upon leaving the Blue

156

Room for a stroll through the rest of the rooms.

The other handout, a tri-fold brochure touting the treasures of Baleroy, is also generously spiced with the mansion's otherworldly attributes:

•During the past twenty years, the development of psychic phenomena has been increasingly evident. Deceased residents and others of the past connected with things in the collection have been seen and heard in Baleroy's halls and chambers

•One of the apparitions—observed by several people—seen at Baleroy in recent times was the figure of Thomas Jefferson

•It is in this [second floor] hallway that a likeness of a former occupant dressed in black and supporting herself with a cane has been observed by visitors to the estate

With these brochures as our menus, we settled in to savor the feast of the supernatural we were about to be served.

Named after a chateau in the Loire Valley of France, Baleroy has been the subject of numerous television, theatrical, and literary investigations and presentations, and has been called "quite possibly the most haunted house in America."

"During one investigation," Easby said, "a camera crew was filming. We asked if my mother was in our presence. Well, the light above the bookcase in the Blue Room blinked. It scared the camera crewmen, and they decided to leave the room quickly and work outside!"

Easby's family heritage is dear to him, and essential to the ghost stories.

"My mother died before my father, and she came back

to him, into his room, and stood by his bed twice. The nurse also saw her. She was wearing a sort of night gown," Easby related.

His mother has been seen several times. "Two or three of my friends have seen her," he said.

Another individual close to Meade has made its presence known at Baleroy.

"My brother, Stevey, died at eleven years old," Easby said. "He's been seen several times at the window. Once we took a picture of a chair and a small figure appeared in the photo. We think it was my brother."

Actually, it was a contractor working on a project in the "Grotto," the shaded, landscaped yard between the mansion and the carriage house.

As the worker labored below, something at a second-floor rear window caught his eye. He looked up to find the face of a young boy staring down at him from the second-floor landing of the house.

While no ghosts seem to roam between the fountains and gardens of the Grotto, a quite interesting intruder rolls its way into the property from time to time—the ghost car.

Mostly at night, but occasionally in broad daylight, the phantom motorcar wends its way through the slim driveway which courses between high stone walls.

"We don't see it," Easby said, "but very often we'll hear a car go by in the driveway. It goes right by the window. Many people have heard it, and we look, but there's no car there."

There's no reasonable explanation, as the driveway is not a thoroughfare. It ends in a cul-de-sac at the Carriage House (in which is a 1935 Packard sports car, a 1953 Packard, and a Rolls Royce once owned by the Ali Kahn and Zsa Zsa Gabor).

Easby treats the "ghost car" phenomenon with characteristic good humor. "My theory is that it's someone in my family coming back to check to see if I'm behaving," he chuckled.

Despite the fact that Easby shares his beloved home with seemingly countless ghosts, he is quite comfortable, even though the spirits sometime become demonstrative.

Wall hangings have fallen from walls, and one particular painting was flung some 15 feet by an unseen force from its wall.

"The amazing thing," Easby related, "is that when a painting flies off a wall, the nail remains tight in the wall and the wire on the painting remains unbroken. So, we're very baffled by what lifts it off the wall and carries it across the room."

The only other hint of malevolence on the part of the ghosts of Baleroy was the time Easby noticed a depression on his bed, as if someone was sitting in it.

Just as he detected the anomaly, he felt something grab his arm with a firm grip. He turned on a light, and whatever was there was gone. Easby said a housekeeper once experienced much the same sensation.

Of the many séances which have been conducted at Baleroy, some have revealed such strong presences that those in attendance have been forewarned of what could be less than friendly spirits in their midst.

"They can be frightening," Easby said of the séances. "One time, an editor came here for one of them, but it became so strong for her that she had to leave the house."

A mysterious form wisps within a staircase at Baleroy. (Photo courtesy of Meade Easby)

One spirit in particular, identified only as Amanda, is the most perplexing. Called a "loose cannon" by Easby, the ghost has thrust door open and slammed them shut, and has been blamed for other events which leads Easby to believe that she has been influenced by a malevolent energy. Still, whatever power she may possess seems to be subdued by the more benign ghosts of the mansion.

At one point in our visit, Easby welcomed us into the most private room in the mansion, the Red Room.

His private study, the room is filled with personal mementos from George Gordon Meade Easby's illustrious career as an artist and cartoonist. Several of his works are considered classics of American patriotic editorial cartoons from World War II. His paintings, some of which are displayed on the walls of a modest third floor gallery, are lovely.

And in the Red Room, upon a large-screen television, Easby played a tape of the TV series, "Sightings," in which Baleroy was once featured.

Easby, several eyewitnesses, and medium Judith Richardson Haines appeared and told their stories.

Ms. Haines was emphatic in her determination that the energy levels in Baleroy are almost overwhelming.

"I'll never forget the first time I walked through the front doors of Baleroy," she said . "The first words out of my mouth were 'My God, I can't believe how many spirits are in this house! Energy absolutely overtook my body!"

That energy has been felt, seen, heard, and even photographed by respected scientific investigators.

As our conversation on the unusual activities in the well-secured, fully-protected home continued, a peculiar sound echoed from a distant room.

It was a squawking, cackling sound which seemed to be unheard by our hosts. Was it the noise from one of the more audible entities of Baleroy? Was it the call from the "great beyond?"

No, it was Timmy.

"He makes the loudest noise made by any living creature," Easby said of his beloved cockatoo.

"It's actually a love call," he pointed out as the cawing continued. "When I got him as a little thing, I had no idea we'd have this!"

Timmy's incessant call became the soundtrack to our pursuit of the ghost stories of the most marvelous old home.

And, even hours into the visit, those stories were not nearly exhausted.

Easby seemed to have a fondness for one story in particular. We shall call it the story of the Monk of Easby.

"It's the kind of thing that happened," Easby said, "that when you tell people about it, they think you're making it up."

But the monk's tale, as all others, is quite true.

"I was in bed, but I don't sleep all night very well. I stay awake a lot, and the time this happened, I'm certain I wasn't dreaming.

"I saw a monk, dressed in a beige robe, appear in the corner of my room."

Even the man who has become somewhat blasé with the ghosts of his manor had to compose himself when he spoke of the monk in the beige robe, and what transpired in his ghostly wake.

"I had been thinking of a little business deal–should I

Many ectoplasmic images have been captured on film at Baleroy. (Photos courtesy of Meade Easby)

do it or shouldn't I? Then, the monk spoke: 'NO, Mr. Easby! NO!'

"Then, the monk dissolved," Easby continued, and added that he reasoned the monk came with the strong suggestion he not enter into the business venture.

"So I didn't," he said.

Easby found out later that had he done the deal, he would have lost a sizable sum of money.

But the monk's tale had not yet reached its conclusion. Sometime later, Easby was touring Great Britain and made a stop at Easby Abbey, the ancestral home of the Easby family.

There, he learned that at that abbey–and only at that abbey, Easby Abbey–monks have, for centuries, dressed in beige habits.

The spirits have led Meade Easby to unexpected finds and minor fortunes on several occasions.

Once, during a séance, a visitor from the "other side" suggested he search the rafters in the attic. He did, and found a valuable pair of candlesticks his mother had hidden many years before.

And, Easby believes it was his mother's spirit who led him to another more significant find–a document stashed in a handsome cabinet in the Blue Room.

Through a series of inexplicable events Easby attributed to his mother's ghost he discovered the document, which contained information from a deceased great uncle.

Easby verified the declarations on the papers, jumped through the legal hoops, and claimed a rightful, and large, inheritance.

"I didn't tell the lawyers how I had found it," Easby quipped. "He probably would have had me locked up!"

While Easby seems at times flippant about those who dwell in Baleroy's other plane, he is actually quite respectful to them.

"I want them to stay," he says in all seriousness. "I like them."

Has it been a lifelong respect and recognition of the ghosts? Has he always believed that he lived among his (usually) invisible entities?

"Well, I have to believe now," he said.

But, he added something which caught this ghost story-hunter off guard.

"Originally, I was brought up to not believe in any of this," he said. "But when they surround you, and with what happens here, one has to believe.

"When I was a young boy, my father once said to me that there's no such thing as ghosts.

"But then, he found out. He met the ghosts of Baleroy.

"He actually left me a note, to be opened upon the event of his death. In that note, he said that he had seen the ghosts, and I would, too."

In that letter from beyond the grave, Easby's father told his heir to not be afraid of those ghosts.

With his own indomitable spirit and his own boundless energy and understanding, George Gordon Meade Easby shall never disappoint his dear, departed father.

⋆⋙⋆

The painting on the right once flew off the wall and landed some 15 feet away—one of many unexplained incidents at the Baleroy estate in Chestnut Hill.

Elusive Spirits

There are times that try the ghost story writer's soul.

The most vexing are the times that a call or visit is made at a particular place which has strong legends and/or ghost stories attached to it.

A cordial request is made to record those legends or stories and include them in the first book ever to chronicle such stories in Philadelphia.

What tries the soul is the terse, almost indignant refusal from the director of the attraction or museum or the owner of the property to share the story.

The owner of private property has every right to reject the proposition. Of this there is no argument.

But, several properties which receive public funds through grants, tax money, or admissions have their stories—of this we are certain—and their perhaps oversensitive curators or caretakers flatly refuse to acknowledge them, and sometimes offer no reason why.

Unfortunately, much valuable folklore and many legends which have been passed on through generations may be lost in time and in the lack of imagination and understanding of certain skeptics or sociopolitical machinations which result in the death of legends.

These items cannot, however, be lost or denied after

they have been made a matter of public record.

Take, for example, one of Philadelphia's truly magnificent mansions, The Woodlands.

Although at least one individual formerly active in the administration of the property acknowledged the time-honored ghost tales in and around the mansion, an attempt to retrieve these stories during the research for this book proved fruitless.

But those who now maintain the property need look no farther than their own files to discover that there are some very interesting stories of very unusual occurrences in the long history of The Woodlands.

Laced with secret passageways and high above the Schuylkill River at the foot of 40th Street in West Philadelphia, The Woodlands was once the 600-acre estate of William Hamilton, grandson of Andrew Hamilton, the prototype "Philadelphia Lawyer" and supervisor of the construction of what is now Independence Hall.

Built in 1790, the mansion is in the southwestern corner of Woodlands Cemetery, which was established in 1840 with a simple philosophy: "...removing the dead from the midst of the dense population of our cities and placing them in operation with the beautiful works of nature."

Among those buried in the cemetery are Joseph Campbell (of the soup company), Anthony J. Drexel (of the university), Samuel D. Gross, M.D. (of the clinic), Ebenezer Maxwell (of the Germantown mansion), Rembrandt Peale (of the paintings), and Anthony Biddle (of the millions of dollars).

There are, according to an 1891 Philadelphia *Times* article about the property, "many legends which cling about the old mansion."

• PHILADELPHIA GHOST STORIES •

As late as 1996, in a publication about ghosts which was published by the Valley Forge Convention and Visitors Bureau, one of those legends was recalled.

It is a story the *Times* said had "a most superstitious flavor."

"One night," the article stated, "it is said that the family were aroused by the howling of the several watch dogs at the stables–the animals rushing around the house, greenhouses and outbuildings, making the woods and shrubbery echo with their dismal wailings.

"The members of the family awakened the servants and made a thorough examination of the house, but failed to find any thief or intruder.

"Early the next morning a messenger from the city brought the news that a member of the family had died at almost the exact time of the prophetic howling of the dogs."

Even more interesting for the purposes of this book is a sentence in yet another article about The Woodlands in the June 14, 1891 *Times*, an which flies in the face of those who choose now to reject a notion which should instead add a certain character to the property.

The statement, unsubstantiated in the subsequent story, was simple and tantalizing:

"The old mansion had the reputation of being haunted."

By whom...where...how...of course, we may never know.

It is interesting to note that the senior Mr. Hamilton (Andrew) once inherited an alleged "haunted house" in Philadelphia.

According to Watson's *Annals of Philadelphia*, "On the northeast corner of Walnut and Fifth Streets once stood a house very generally called the 'haunted house' because of Mr. B having there killed his wife.

"He gave the property to Hamilton to purge him from his sins by pleading his acquittal at the bar.

"It long remained empty from the dread of its invisible guest."

Many such a house has fallen to "progress" as Philadelphia the village grew into a town, and then into a city.

Throughout that city are ghost stories and haunted places which remain elusive because their essences have been dimmed by time or snuffed out by skeptics.

Let us now roam the streets and roads of Philadelphia and visit with some of those entities in some of those places.

Goblins at Schuylkill Falls

A tempting tidbit from the dusty attic of the city's treasure house of history tells of a ghost in the old home of Revolutionary War general and Pennsylvania's first governor, Thomas Mifflin.

Once located near the "falls," on the left bank of the Schuylkill River, the gray stone building was purchased by Mifflin in 1783. The estate was named "Fonthill."

The property passed to a French bachelor, Jacob G. Koch, after Mifflin's death in 1800. As early as then, rumors circulated that Fonthill was haunted.

It was certainly haunted, as it were, with intrigue. Said to be a rendezvous spot for Continental army scouts and a hideaway for what British Gen. Howe called "rebel lookouts," secret passageways and tunnels ran through the property and house.

Gen. Howe ordered the place set on fire because of its

suspected connection with the "rebels," but it was rebuilt in short order.

Thomas Mifflin was said to have been a rather difficult and complex man. More than one reliable source of the day portrayed his wife as having nearly lost her mind trying to cope with his bouts of anger and, what one charitable account called "inconsistencies."

By the middle of the 19th century, a story began to spread around Schuylkill Falls that Mrs. Mifflin's ghost could regularly be seen, dressed in a rustling gray silk dress, gliding down the corridors, looking out the windows, and venturing into the yard and onto the roads which surrounded Fonthill.

An article in the Philadelphia *Times* in 1879 expanded that story when it noted the deplorable condition of the decaying old mansion ("...a drowsy peace has fallen upon Mifflin mansion...").

"It was seldom that anyone tried to live in it," the article said, "and none stayed more than a few weeks or month."

The story added a cryptic note to the ghostly history of Fonthill:

"And now," the writer concluded his or her story, "in place of the gentle shade of the unhappy Mrs. Mifflin, goblins of monstrous shape old their horrible orgies around the old house, which is now chiefly given over to their unearthly revels."

Above the highway, rising bold,
The pillared Mifflin house behold.
Where men and dames of high degree
Were often wont of old to be.

171

• PHILADELPHIA GHOST STORIES •

Come shuddering now the stories told
Of ghostly figures strutting bold;
Of dark recess and double floor,
And never-shutting chamber door;
Of noises strange and flashing light,
Oft heard and seen at dead of night

Mills' *Poem of the Schuylkill*

━━

Skeletons on the Schuylkill?

Another bane of the ghost story hunter is the trick headlines often employed in newspapers of the last century. The editors of the Philadelphia *Times*, which was a valuable source of early ghost stories, seemed quite adept at the practice..

Witness the teasing banner in the *Times* of June 27, 1890: THE GHOST-LIKE BOATMAN.

The headline obviously stopped the researcher dead, so to speak, in his tracks.

But, it was only a setup for a letdown.

It turned out to be the revisitation of a 1784 story of a mysterious boat seen floating down the Schuylkill River, near the Fairmount Ferry just after midnight.

"Soon after, it began to be whispered that the occupant of the skiff was not of this world, and the rumor spread that skeletons were traveling along the silent highway of the Schuylkill."

It was later discovered that the mystery was perpetrated by a young couple simply looking to have some fun with the superstitious citizenry.

Of Fairy Rock, the Phantom Coach, and the Galloping Ghost of Allens Lane

Legends and superstitions have been abundant throughout Philadelphia's history.

In the 18th century, folks would beware of the "Phantom Coach" which would ramble through the streets of town pulled by an invisible demon.

In the coach was its ghostly occupant, "Deemed," an old narrative claimed "to have died with unkind feelings toward one dependent on him."

That tale seemed to persist in retelling through the turn of the nineteenth century.

Allens Lane, which extends from the Wissahickon Valley to Germantown Avenue, is one roadway upon which another ghost is said to gallop.

The story was told as early as 1775 of a Colonial soldier who sped on his horse along the lane, clutching his severed head.

According to some sources, the headless soldier's spirit was seen as recently as 1986—and then, by two Philadelphia police officers!

A popular legend around the turn of the twentieth century was centered on "Fairy Rock," a large boulder adjacent to Old York Road at Rock Run Creek in the old neighborhood of Branchtown.

The rock got its name from a superstition that a fairy inhabited a crevasse under the rock. Some folks in that part of town claimed they could hear the sound of someone spinning yarn coming from the narrow cave and said it was the work of the fairy.

The charming legend may have had some basis in

reality, however.

Not far from Fairy Rock, in another cave, once lived a man named Benjamin Lay, who made his home in what was known as "Hermit's Cave."

It was he, pragmatists said, who was doing the spinning, and it was that sound that echoed through the caverns, not a that of a "fairy" at all.

The Hovering Girl of Frankford

Another mysterious tale which has all but vanished in the mist of time is that of the ghost of a young Quaker girl who committed suicide at "Chalkley Hall" in Frankford.

A vague reference to the ghost, which was said to "hover in the night" at Chalkley, was made and never further explained, in a 1937 guide to Philadelphia which was published by the Works Progress Administration (WPA).

Strange Doings at Fireman's Hall

If legends and important pieces of folklore are to survive in the highly-technological and scientific twenty-first century, they will do so through a withering sensitivity known as imagination and a dying art known as storytelling.

In the author's broad search for ghost stories in Philadelphia, few stones were left unturned (although the research team could still only scratch the surface of the wealth of haunted places in Philadelphia).

Down in Old City, at Second and Quarry Streets, is the city fire station dedicated to education and history, "Fireman's Hall."

And in its brochure is a description of the fine attraction's displays and exhibits, including a recreated living quarters of old-time firefighters.

So real is this recreation, says the brochure, "It is as if

the ghosts of those early stalwarts still inhabit the room!"

Well, Henry J. Magee, do they?

Magee is a fourth-generation Philadelphia firefighter, and the pride he has in that service is quite obvious. He also has Irish blood running through his veins, so a bit of the *shanachian* tends to come to the fore.

When we dropped by to ask about any spirits which may indeed inhabit the old fire station, museum curator (and active city firefighter) Magee shrugged and told us the only unexplainable thing that happens in the building is a the fairly regular occurrence of the elevator moving itself from floor to floor on its own.

"We say it's 'Old Ben' doing it," Magee said. "We can't explain it away or figure it out, so we just blame it on Ben—as in Ben Franklin, who started the fire department in 1736."

Is it the ghost of Ben Franklin? Probably not. But does even the most remote possibility that a phantom's finger presses that elevator button add a certain character to Fireman's Hall? Probably so.

The "Pretty Lady" of the Powel House

Along "Mansion Row" in the 200 block of South Third Street is the Powel House, where Samuel (Philadelphia's first mayor) and Elizabeth Powel hosted the likes of Lafayette, Washington, Franklin, and anybody who was anybody in Colonial Philadelphia.

Truly one of the most elegant homes in the city, the Powel House is also, according to sightings made by former residents and reported in a 1965 story in the *Bulletin* truly haunted..

Edwin Coutant Moore told a reporter that he had seen two young officers coming toward him as he was descending a staircase in the front of the house.

Moore speculated that one of the officers, clad in a blue uniform, may have been the spirit of the Marquis de Lafayette.

Does the ghost of the Marquis de Lafayette haunt the Powel House?

Moore, a respected historian, reported other odd occurrences in the historic home, and was convinced the spacious Georgian townhouse was inhabited by residents on the "other side."

Mrs. Moore also believed in and fully accepted the existence of spirits in the Powel House.

She, too, had seen a spirit there.

Her experience took place in the drawing room, where she caught a glimpse of what she described as a "pretty lady" in a lavender and beige dress.

Mrs. Moore watched in awe as the ghostly young woman fanned herself and tapped her foot.

As mysteriously as the spirit appeared, it vanished.

The Bride of the City Tavern

For those who seek to combine fine dining in a candle-lit, historic site in the heart of the city with a bit of ghost hunting, the City Tavern at Second and Walnut Streets fills the bill.

The original City Tavern grew as the nation grew. Opened in 1773, the three-story tavern became a meeting place for the likes of Jefferson, Adams, and Washington–and every other "founding father" who toiled in Philadelphia during the formative years of the United States. John Adams once wrote to a friend and mentioned the City Tavern as "the most genteel tavern in America."

In 1774, members of the First Continental Congress convened there, and in 1787 the Constitutional Convention concluded with a banquet there.

Now an atmospheric, charming restaurant in which staff dress in Colonial style and food and beverage selections reflect early America, the City Tavern still serves as a popular gathering spot.

The present building is actually a down-to-the-last-nail recreation of the original, rebuilt by the National Park Service to exacting specifications of the 1773 structure, which was destroyed by fire in 1854.

And it is from the flames of that fire that the ghost of the City Tavern has emerged.

The story is told by staff members at the tavern, and all swear it to be true.

A beautiful young woman and handsome young man were to marry in the tavern on a day in 1854.

The groom-to-be met with his chums in the first-floor pub while his bride and her party gathered upstairs.

Lighting in the tavern at the time was by lantern and candle. As the bride's maids were putting the final touches on her trousseau, the unthinkable happened.

The train of her elegant gown was said to be some ten feet in length. As the women fussed with her veil and gown, no one noticed that a candle had tipped over and touched off a fire in a curtain on a window at the other end of the room.

Fire safety codes and awareness not being what they are today, the curtain slowly but steadily burned as the bridal party went about its business.

Soon, though, a pungent smoke drifted through the room, down the stairs, and onto the main floor.

Upstairs, it was too late. Flames were rapidly spreading, and the women were trapped. There was no escape.

Downstairs, the prospective groom and his aides made a desperate attempt to ascend the stairs and rescue the women.

They could not fight through the thick smoke and flames which were cascading down the steps. The bride and her friends were doomed.

It was that fire which caused so much damage to the City Tavern in 1854 which resulted in its ultimate demolition—only to rise triumphantly and in its exact form 120 years later.

But to this day, those who work and many who dine in the tavern say they have seen or felt the presence of that bride as her spirit still roams the corridors, dining rooms, and staircases of the City Tavern.

A sad ghost, the bride causes no damage, but has been known to make her presence known during certain functions at the tavern.

And several photographs taken in the Long Room, where modern weddings are performed and receptions are held, have been developed only to show the phantom face of a fair maiden staring faintly into the camera from its eternal imprisonment.

And, There are More...

...many more ghost stories within the borders of Philadelphia.

The ca. 1743 Belmont Mansion in Fairmount Park holds within it spirits which have made themselves known and have caught visitors and guides unaware.

One woman said the energy in the mansion was so strong that she actually responded vocally to what she believed was the audible call of the ghost.

Another Fairmount Park mansion, Mount Pleasant, has had its share of incidents. One sent a security guard scurrying after he witnessed what he described as a pair of red slippers descending a staircase–with no *visible* body attached to them!

Some say the Civil War Library and Museum on Pine Street is inhabited by several soldiers who play a ghostly card game in the Lincoln Room on the second floor.

While the museum's curator, Steve Wright, concedes that there is a certain "presence" about the building, and that he and others have heard what seems to be "walking around" sounds upstairs, the story of the card-playing soldiers (obtained by the authors from a site on the internet) was news to him.

However, Dale Biever, registrar at the museum, did have a very strange incident take place there in the late 1980s.

"I don't believe in any of this," he said, "but I did have something very strange occur here.

"I was working on items belonging to General Grant," the man who identifies and catalogs artifacts for the museum continued. "I had a large work table set up on the third floor.

"His uniform was there, his sword, his epaulets, bandana–and a silver cigar case.

"I'm working away on this stuff, and I smelled cigar smoke. Well, of course, smoking in the museum is a no-no. There was nobody else on the third floor.

"About 20 minutes later, I went downstairs. The secretary was there, and I told her that nobody's supposed to be smoking in the building. She said no one's been there.

"I went back upstairs, and I literally sniffed everything–down to the armpit of Ulysses S. Grant's uniform. I smelled nothing."

Biever also told of a visitor to the museum who took a photograph of a painting of Pickett's Charge in the battle of Gettysburg. When the photo was developed, the face of a young man appeared—a face which was not in the painting!

In the chapel of the Chestnut Hill Academy, a renowned prep school situated in the former Wissahickon Inn on W. Willow Grove Ave., a school historical publication mentions a ghost who occupies space in the school chapel.

Researchers compiling information for a history of the academy came across the mention of the time a cleaning woman was distracted by something odd in one of the back pews. It was, the story goes, a man sitting there, *holding his head in his lap!*

The filmy form of woman dressed in a long gown has been seen in the Physick House on South Fourth Street, and there are dusty tales which tell of a ghost who wanders aimlessly through Rittenhouse Square every Friday at dusk—the ghost, they say, of a young woman who was stood up at the altar in the 1920s and died as an "old maid" in a home which overlooks the square.

There are also countless stories gleaned not from newspaper morgues, historical societies, libraries, or in historic buildings or neighborhoods.

They are the stories told by everyday people who have had brushes with entities and incidents they simply could not reason away or rationalize.

For example: The man who smelled perfume, watched as doors opened on their own, and heard bumps in the night at an old home in Overbrook; or the ten-year old girl who lives in a 120-year old home on Indian Queen Lane in East Falls, where footsteps can be heard, doors creak open after being shut tight, and an invisible force field often seems to wrap around the residents and visitors.

In the author's home area of the Pennsylvania "Dutch Country," there is one saying—one answer—which can be given when all else fails, when all reasonable explanations have been exhausted.

The "Dutchman" shrugs, and with a certain sense of frustration, quips, "Well, it *makes you wonder!*"

Many of the stories in this book, on many psychic and sensory levels, truly do *make one wonder*.

And when *wonder*, when *legend*, when a *damned good ghost story* become things of the past, perhaps society has little to look forward to in the future.

ABOUT THE AUTHOR

A native of Reading, Pennsylvania, Adams is a veteran broadcaster on radio station WEEU there, and is also chief travel correspondent for the Reading *Eagle* newspaper.

Charlie Adams has written 20 books on ghost stories, folklore, shipwrecks and train wrecks in New Jersey, Pennsylvania, Delaware, and New York. His books have never been out of print since 1982.

He is a member of the board of trustees of the Historical Society of Berks County, Pa., and is also chairman of its publications committee. He is past president of the Reading Public Library, and very active in civic affairs in his home county.

ABOUT THE RESEARCH TEAM
THE PHILADELPHIA GHOST HUNTERS ALLIANCE

Husband and wife Sharon M. and Lewis B. Gerew II are Philadelphians who, in 1997, founded the Philadelphia Ghost Hunters Alliance.

Both graduates of Abraham Lincoln High School, Sharon and Lew share many interests, including the investigation of the paranormal.

A state-certified Nurse Assistant, Sharon said she had her first experience with spirits when she was four years old, and has been fascinated by the subject ever since.

Lew, a radiologic technologist, has also had personal experiences with ghosts, and says ghost hunting is one of the "passions" of his life.

DAVID J. SEIBOLD

Dave Seibold is the Chief Executive Officer of Exeter House Books, and has shared much of the research conducted in the publication of books written by Charles J. Adams III.

The Senior Account Executive at radio station WEEU in Reading, Dave is also an experienced fisherman and charter boat captain. He divides his time between homes in Flying Hills, Pa., and Barnegat Light, N.J., and is an award-winning ballroom dancer.

ACKNOWLEDGMENTS

In addition to the obvious sources and references mentioned in this book, the authors would like to recognize and thank the following for providing assistance and information which led to the compilation of the preceding stories.

MAGAZINES and NEWSPAPERS

Philadelphia *Press*, Philadelphia *Times*, *Philadelphia Inquirer*, *The Philadelphia Evening Bulletin*, *The Public Ledger*, *The New York Times*, *Reading Eagle*, *National Enquirer*, *Philadelphia Weekly*, *American Literature*, *The Sunday Mercury*, *Philadelphia City Paper*, *South Philadelphia Review Chronicle*, The *Courier-Post*, *Pennsylvania* magazine, *Associated Press*.

BOOKS

The WPA Guide to Philadelphia, 1988 (Originally published as *Philadelphia: A Guide to the Nation's Birthplace*, 1937); *Rebels and Gentlemen: Philadelphia in the Age of Franklin*, Carl and Jessica Bridenbaugh, 1962; *Watson's Annals of Philadelphia*, Vol. 1, John F. Watson, 1887; *The Ocean Almanac*, Robert Hendrickson, 1984; *The Encyclopedia of the Occult* Lewis Spence, 1988; *A Guide Book of Art, Architecture, and Historic Interests in Pennsylvania*, A. Margaretta Archambault, Editor, 1924; *Fort Mifflin: Valiant Defender of the Delaware*, John W. Jackson, 1986; *Walking Tours of Historic Philadelphia*, John Francis Marion, 1974; *Christopher Morley's Philadelphia*, Ken Kalfus, Editor, 1990; *Philadelphia Architecture: A Guide to the City*, John Andrew Gallery, Editor, 1994; *Philadelphia: The Place and the People*, Agnes Repplier, 1899; *Azimov Laughs Again*, Isaac Azimov, 1992; *Reminiscences of a Very Old Man*, John Sartain, 1899; *History of Old Germantown*, 1907; *The History of an Old Philadelphia Land Title*, John Frederick Lewis, 1934; *Germantown 1683-1933*, Edward W. Hocker, 1933; *Ghosts of the Rich and Famous*, Arthur Myers; *The Wissahickon*, T.A. Daly, 1922; *Philadelphia Almanac and Citizens' Manual*, 1994 and 1995, The Library Company of Philadelphia.

INDIVIDUALS, ORGANIZATIONS, ETC.

Detailed Inventory of Naval Shore Facilities, 1992; Historic Naval Ships Assn., Office of Naval Research, Henry Graham Ashmead's "Newspaper Cuttings About Pennsylvania History," Valley Forge Convention and Visitors Bureau, Ron Avery, Randy Giancaterino, Peggy Miller, Chestnut Hill Business Association, The Free Library of Philadelphia, the Historical Society of Pennsylvania, Reading Public Library, Penn State Berks-Lehigh Valley Thun Library, The Buffalo and Erie County Naval and Servicemen's Park, Pennsylvania Department of Commerce, City of Philadelphia Fire Department, Friends of the Wissahickon, Germantown Historical Society, Robert Yrigoyen.

MOTION PICTURE

"The Philadelphia Experiment" (1985)

All photographs by the author, unless otherwise noticed. Vintage post cards from the collection of the author.

To T.